Volume 2

Lift the Lid on Brand-New Dinner Ideas for Your Slow Cooker

THE MORE you experience the ease of preparing foods in the slow cooker—and taste how delicious those dishes can be—the more you want to use that handy kitchen appliance.

You see that slow cookers give you not just family-pleasing main courses, but also impressive appetizers…hearty soups and stews…satisfying side dishes…sensational sandwiches…thirst-quenching beverages…super snacks and even delectable desserts.

And you discover that slow cookers come in handy for just about every occasion, from sit-down suppers on busy weekdays and brunch on lazy weekends to dinner parties, holiday feasts, potlucks, church activities, casual gatherings for friends and special family celebrations.

That's why anyone who appreciates slow cooking is certain to love *Best of Country Slow Cooker Recipes Volume 2*. This brand-new collection contains even more of the best slow cooker recipes—230 in all—shared by busy cooks like you from across the country.

As in Volume 1, every scrumptious dish in this jam-packed book was prepared and tested by the home economists in the *Taste of Home* Test Kitchen—and many include a gorgeous full-color photo that shows you the completed recipe. So you can rest assured that the food you serve your family will be a winner every time.

This indispensable book follows the same helpful format of the first edition. Because cooking times for slow-cooked foods can range from all day to just a few hours, we've prominently highlighted the time with each recipe so you can easily choose dishes that suit your schedule.

You'll also find a complete listing of recipes organized by cooking time on page 107 of the index. (If you'd like to select dishes based on food category or ingredient, simply turn to the index on page 109.) And we've featured plenty of useful recipe hints, tips and ideas scattered throughout the chapters.

So go ahead—page through *Best of Country Slow Cooker Recipes Volume 2* and uncover hundreds more of the tastiest, most popular family dishes—all straight from the slow cooker!

Editor: Michelle Bretl
Art Director: Nancy Novak
Executive Editor/Books: Heidi Reuter Lloyd
Senior Editor/Books: Mark Hagen
Layout Designers: Emma Acevedo, Catherine Fletcher
Proofreader: Linne Bruskewitz
Editorial Assistant: Barb Czysz
Food Editor: Janaan Cunningham
Associate Food Editors: Coleen Martin, Diane Werner
Senior Recipe Editor: Sue A. Jurack
Recipe Editor: Mary King

Food Photographers: Rob Hagen, Dan Roberts, Jim Wieland
Associate Photographer: Lori Foy
Food Stylists: Sue Draheim, Sarah Thompson
Set Stylists: Sue Myers, Jennifer Bradley Vent, Stephanie Marchese
Associate Set Stylist: Melissa Haberman
Photo Studio Coordinator: Suzanne Kern
Creative Director: Ardyth Cope
Senior Vice President/Editor in Chief: Catherine Cassidy
President: Barbara Newton
Founder: Roy Reiman

© 2006 Reiman Media Group, Inc.
5400 S. 60th St., Greendale WI 53129
International Standard Book Number: 0-89821-509-9
Library of Congress Control Number: 2006926872
All rights reserved.
Printed in China.
Second Printing, September 2006

Pictured on front cover: Sweet-and-Sour Chicken (p. 66)
Pictured on back cover: Sweet 'n' Sour Sausage (p. 88)
and Barbecued Beef Brisket (p. 49)

Best of Country Slow Cooker

RECIPES

Volume 2

Makes a Great Gift!

To order additional copies of the *Best of Country Slow Cooker Recipes Volume 2* book, specify item number 36208 and send $15.99 (plus $4.99 shipping/insured delivery for one book, $5.50 for two or more) to: Country Store, Suite 8885, P.O. Box 990, Greendale WI 53129-0990. To order by credit card, call toll-free 1-800/558-1013 or visit our Web site at *www.reimanpub.com*.

Snacks & Beverages

Barbecue Sausage Bites (p. 9)

Chapter 1

Hot Bacon Cheese Dip

Hot Bacon Cheese Dip

(Pictured above)

Cook Time: 2 Hours

Suzanne Whitaker, Knoxville, Tennessee

I've tried several appetizers before, but this one is a guaranteed people-pleaser. The thick dip has lots of bacon flavor.

  2 packages (8 ounces *each*) cream cheese, cubed
  4 cups (16 ounces) shredded cheddar cheese
  1 cup half-and-half cream
  2 teaspoons Worcestershire sauce
  1 teaspoon dried minced onion
  1 teaspoon prepared mustard
 16 bacon strips, cooked and crumbled
Tortilla chips *or* French bread slices

In a 1-1/2-qt. slow cooker, combine the first six ingredients. Cover and cook for 2 hours or until cheeses are melted, stirring occasionally. Just before serving, stir in bacon. Serve warm with tortilla chips or bread. **Yield:** 4 cups.

Pizza Dip

Cook Time: 1-1/2 to 2 Hours

Sara Nowacki, Franklin, Wisconsin

Everybody loves this sensational dip. If you have any left over, spoon it on toasted English muffins for a sandwich.

  2 packages (8 ounces *each*) cream cheese, cubed
  1 can (14 ounces) pizza sauce
  1 package (8 ounces) sliced pepperoni, chopped
  1 can (3.8 ounces) chopped ripe olives, drained
  2 cups (8 ounces) shredded part-skim mozzarella cheese
Bagel chips *or* garlic toast

Place the cream cheese in a 3-qt. slow cooker. Combine the pizza sauce, pepperoni and olives; pour over cream cheese. Top with mozzarella cheese. Cover and cook on low for 1-1/2 to 2 hours or until cheese is melted. Stir; serve warm with bagel chips or garlic toast. **Yield:** 5-1/2 cups.

Tangy Pork Meatballs

Serve in Slow Cooker

Katie Koziolek, Hartland, Minnesota

Yuletide buffet "grazers" stampede for these meatballs! The mouth-watering morsels go so fast, I often make several batches at once. Adding Liquid Smoke to the tasty, homemade barbecue sauce gives it even more flavor.

  2 eggs, beaten
2/3 cup dried bread crumbs
  2 tablespoons dried minced onion
  2 teaspoons seasoned salt
  2 pounds ground pork

SAUCE:
1-1/2 cups ketchup
1 can (8 ounces) tomato sauce
3 tablespoons Worcestershire sauce
2 to 3 tablespoons cider vinegar
2 teaspoons Liquid Smoke, optional

In a bowl, combine the eggs, bread crumbs, onion and salt. Crumble pork over mixture and mix well. Shape into 3/4-in. balls; place on a greased 15-in. x 10-in. x 1-in. baking pan. Bake at 400° for 15 minutes or until the meat is no longer pink.

Meanwhile, in a large saucepan, combine sauce ingredients. Simmer, uncovered, for 10 minutes, stirring occasionally. Add meatballs. Serve in a slow cooker. **Yield:** about 7-1/2 dozen.

Beer Cheese Fondue

(Pictured below)

Serve in Slow Cooker

Chrystie Wear, Greensboro, North Carolina

This thick fondue originated in my kitchen when I didn't have the ingredients I needed for the recipe I initially planned to make. Served with bread, it has become a staple.

1 loaf (20 inches) French bread, cubed
1/4 cup chopped onion
1 teaspoon minced garlic
1 tablespoon butter
1 cup beer *or* nonalcoholic beer
4 cups (16 ounces) shredded cheddar cheese
1 tablespoon all-purpose flour
2 to 4 tablespoons half-and-half cream

Place bread cubes in a single layer in an ungreased 15-in. x 10-in. x 1-in. baking pan. Bake at 450° for 5-7 minutes or until lightly crisp, stirring twice.

Beer Cheese Fondue

Cranberry Apple Cider

Meanwhile, in a small saucepan, saute onion and garlic in butter until tender. Stir in beer. Bring to a boil; reduce heat to medium-low. Toss cheese and flour; stir into saucepan until melted. Stir in 2 tablespoons cream.

Transfer to a small ceramic fondue pot or slow cooker; keep warm. Add additional cream if fondue thickens. Serve with toasted bread cubes. **Yield:** about 3 cups.

Cranberry Apple Cider

(Pictured above)

Cook Time: 2 Hours

Jennifer Naboka, North Plainfield, New Jersey

I like to start this soothing cider in the slow cooker before my husband goes hunting. Then he can fill his thermos and take it with him out into the cold.

4 cups water
4 cups apple juice
1 can (12 ounces) frozen apple juice concentrate, thawed
1 medium apple, peeled and sliced
1 cup fresh *or* frozen cranberries
1 medium orange, peeled and sectioned
1 cinnamon stick

In a slow cooker, combine all ingredients; mix well. Cover and cook on low for 2 hours or until the cider reaches the desired temperature. Discard the cinnamon stick. If desired, remove the fruit with a slotted spoon before serving. **Yield:** 10 servings (about 2-1/2 quarts).

Hot Spiced Lemon Drink

1 package (2-1/2 ounces) thinly sliced dried
   beef, chopped
1/4 cup chopped green onions
2 teaspoons ground mustard
1 loaf (1 pound) French bread, cubed

In a saucepan, heat milk and cream cheese over medium heat; stir until smooth. Stir in beef, onions and mustard; heat through. Transfer to a fondue pot or slow cooker; keep warm. Serve with bread cubes. **Yield:** about 4 cups.

Paddy's Reuben Dip

(Pictured below)

Cook Time: 2 Hours

Mary Jane Kimmes, Hastings, Minnesota

This dip tastes just like the popular Reuben sandwich. Even when I double the recipe, I end up with an empty dish.

4 packages (4-1/2 ounces *each*) deli corned
   beef, finely chopped
1 package (8 ounces) cream cheese, cubed
1 can (8 ounces) sauerkraut, rinsed and
   drained
1 cup (8 ounces) sour cream
1 cup (4 ounces) shredded Swiss cheese
Rye bread or crackers

In a mini slow cooker, combine the first five ingredients. Cover and cook on low for 2 hours or until

Hot Spiced Lemon Drink

(Pictured above)

Cook Time: 2 to 3 Hours

Mandy Wright, Springville, Utah

I received this recipe from a lady in our church who is an excellent cook. We really enjoy the sweet-and-tangy flavor of this warm citrus punch.

2-1/2 quarts water
2 cups sugar
1-1/2 cups orange juice
1/2 cup plus 2 tablespoons lemon juice
1/4 cup pineapple juice
1 cinnamon stick (3 inches)
1/2 teaspoon whole cloves

In a 5-qt. slow cooker, combine the water, sugar and juices. Place cinnamon stick and cloves on a double thickness of cheesecloth; bring up corners of cloth and tie with kitchen string to form a bag. Place in slow cooker. Cover and cook on low for 2-3 hours or until heated through. Discard spice bag. **Yield:** about 3 quarts.

Creamy Chipped Beef Fondue

Serve in Slow Cooker

Beth Fox, Lawrence, Kansas

My mother often served fondue on Christmas Eve, and I've since followed that tradition. It's nice to offer a hearty homemade appetizer that requires very little work.

1-1/3 to 1-1/2 cups milk
2 packages (8 ounces *each*) cream cheese,
   cubed

Paddy's Reuben Dip

cheese is melted; stir until blended. Serve warm with bread or crackers. **Yield:** about 4 cups.

Barbecue Sausage Bites

(Pictured at right and on page 4)

Cook Time: 2-1/2 to 3 Hours

Rebekah Randolph, Greer, South Carolina

This sweet-and-tangy appetizer pairs pineapple chunks with three kinds of sausage. I experimented with the amounts of pineapple and barbecue sauce to suit my taste.

- 1 package (1 pound) miniature smoked sausage links
- 3/4 pound fully cooked bratwurst links, cut into 1/2-inch slices
- 3/4 pound fully cooked kielbasa *or* Polish sausage, cut into 1/2-inch slices
- 1 bottle (18 ounces) barbecue sauce
- 2/3 cup orange marmalade
- 1/2 teaspoon ground mustard
- 1/8 teaspoon ground allspice
- 1 can (20 ounces) pineapple chunks, drained

In a 3-qt. slow cooker, combine the sausages. In a small bowl, whisk the barbecue sauce, marmalade, mustard and allspice. Pour over sausage mixture; stir to coat.

   Cover and cook on high for 2-1/2 to 3 hours or until heated through. Stir in pineapple. Serve with toothpicks. **Yield:** 12-14 servings.

Peppered Meatballs

Cook Time: 2 Hours

Darla Schroeder, Stanley, North Dakota

Ground pepper gives these saucy, cheesy meatball bites extra zest. I've prepared them many times as an appetizer at gatherings. But they're so hearty and tasty, I've also served them over noodles as a main course.

- 1/2 cup sour cream
- 2 teaspoons grated Parmesan *or* Romano cheese
- 2 to 3 teaspoons pepper
- 1 teaspoon salt
- 1 teaspoon dry bread crumbs
- 1/2 teaspoon garlic powder
- 1-1/2 pounds ground beef
SAUCE:
- 1 cup (8 ounces) sour cream
- 1 can (10-3/4 ounces) condensed cream of mushroom soup, undiluted
- 2 teaspoons dill weed
- 1/2 teaspoon sugar
- 1/2 teaspoon pepper
- 1/4 teaspoon garlic powder

Barbecue Sausage Bites

In a bowl, combine sour cream and Parmesan cheese. Add pepper, salt, bread crumbs and garlic powder. Crumble meat over mixture and mix well. Shape into 1-in. balls. Place in a greased 15-in. x 10-in. x 1-in. baking pan. Bake at 350° for 20-25 minutes or until no longer pink.

   Transfer meatballs to a slow cooker. Combine the sauce ingredients; pour over meatballs. Cover and cook on high for 2 hours or until heated through. **Yield:** 1-1/2 dozen (2 cups sauce).

Hot Chili Cheese Dip

Cook Time: 4 Hours

Jeanie Carrigan, Madera, California

I simplify party preparation by using my slow cooker to create this thick dip. Guests rave about how good it is.

- 1 medium onion, finely chopped
- 2 garlic cloves, minced
- 2 teaspoons vegetable oil
- 2 cans (15 ounces *each*) chili without beans
- 2 cups salsa
- 2 packages (3 ounces *each*) cream cheese, cubed
- 2 cans (2-1/4 ounces *each*) sliced ripe olives, drained
Tortilla chips

In a skillet, saute onion and garlic in oil until tender. Transfer to a slow cooker. Stir in the chili, salsa, cream cheese and olives. Cover and cook on low for 4 hours or until heated through, stirring occasionally. Stir before serving with tortilla chips. **Yield:** 6 cups.

Warm Spiced Cider Punch

Cook Time: 4 to 5 Hours

Susan Smith, Forest, Virginia

This is a nice warm-up punch—I like to serve it on cold days. The aroma of the simmering cider is wonderful.

> 4 **cups apple cider** *or* **unsweetened apple juice**
> 2-1/4 **cups water**
> 3/4 **cup orange juice concentrate**
> 3/4 **teaspoon ground nutmeg**
> 3/4 **teaspoon ground ginger**
> 3 **whole cloves**
> 2 **cinnamon sticks**
> 4 **orange slices, halved**

In a 3-qt. slow cooker, combine apple cider, water, orange juice concentrate, nutmeg and ginger. Place cloves and cinnamon sticks on a double thickness of cheesecloth. Bring up corners of cloth; tie with string to form a bag. Place bag in slow cooker.

Cover and cook on low for 4-5 hours or until heated through. Remove and discard spice bag. Garnish with orange slices. **Yield:** 8 servings.

Moist 'n' Tender Wings

(Pictured below)

Cook Time: 8 Hours

Sharon Morcilio, Joshua Tree, California

These no-fuss wings are fall-off-the-bone tender. Chili sauce offers a bit of spice while molasses lends a hint of sweetness. They make a great meal with a side dish of rice.

> 25 **whole chicken wings (about 5 pounds)**
> 1 **bottle (12 ounces) chili sauce**
> 1/4 **cup lemon juice**
> 1/4 **cup molasses**
> 2 **tablespoons Worcestershire sauce**
> 6 **garlic cloves, minced**
> 1 **tablespoon chili powder**
> 1 **tablespoon salsa**
> 1 **teaspoon garlic salt**
> 3 **drops hot pepper sauce**

Cut chicken wings into three sections and discard wing tips. Place the wings in a 5-qt. slow cooker. In a bowl, combine the remaining ingredients; pour over chicken. Stir to coat. Cover and cook on low for 8 hours or until chicken is tender. **Yield:** about 4 dozen.

Editor's Note: Five pounds of uncooked chicken wing sections (wingettes) may be substituted for the whole chicken wings. Omit the first step.

Cheesy Pizza Fondue

(Pictured above right)

Cook Time: 4 to 6 Hours

Nel Carver, Moscow, Idaho

I always keep the ingredients for this dip in my kitchen for casual get-togethers. It's great any time of the year.

> 1 **jar (29 ounces) meatless spaghetti sauce**
> 2 **cups (8 ounces) shredded part-skim mozzarella cheese**
> 1/4 **cup shredded Parmesan cheese**
> 2 **teaspoons dried oregano**
> 1 **teaspoon dried minced onion**

Moist 'n' Tender Wings

Cheesy Pizza Fondue

1/4 teaspoon garlic powder
1 unsliced loaf (1 pound) Italian bread,
cut into cubes

In a 1-1/2-qt. slow cooker, combine the spaghetti sauce, cheeses, oregano, onion and garlic powder. Cook for 4-6 hours or until cheeses are melted and sauce is hot. Serve with bread cubes. **Yield:** 12 servings (4 cups).

Zesty Smoked Links

Serve in Slow Cooker

Jackie Boothman, La Grande, Oregon

These flavorful sausages are great when entertaining. The men in my family can't resist them.

1 bottle (12 ounces) chili sauce
1 cup grape jelly
2 tablespoons lemon juice
2 packages (1 pound *each*) miniature
smoked sausage links *and/or* hot dogs

In a large skillet, combine chili sauce, jelly and lemon juice; cook over medium-low heat until jelly is melted. Stir in sausages. Reduce heat; cover and cook for 30 minutes or until heated through, stirring occasionally. Serve immediately or keep warm in a slow cooker. **Yield:** about 32 servings.

Tomato Fondue

Serve in Slow Cooker

Marlene Muckenhirn, Delano, Minnesota

Both the young and young at heart will gobble up this cheesy tomato fondue served with mini hot dogs and bread cubes.

1 garlic clove, halved
1/2 cup condensed tomato soup, undiluted
1-1/2 teaspoons ground mustard
1-1/2 teaspoons Worcestershire sauce
10 slices process cheese (Velveeta), cubed

1/4 to 1/3 cup milk
1 package (16 ounces) miniature hot dogs *or*
smoked sausage, warmed
Cubed French bread

Rub garlic clove over the bottom and sides of a small fondue pot or slow cooker; discard garlic and set fondue pot aside. In a small saucepan, combine the tomato soup, mustard and Worcestershire sauce; heat through. Stir in cheese until melted. Stir in milk; heat through. Transfer to prepared fondue pot and keep warm. Serve with hot dogs and bread cubes. **Yield:** about 1 cup.

Orange Spiced Cider

(Pictured below)

Cook Time: 2 to 3 Hours

Erika Reinhard, Colorado Springs, Colorado

Every time I serve this hot beverage, someone asks for the recipe. Orange juice adds sweetness while red-hot candies are a fun substitute for traditional cinnamon sticks.

4 cups unsweetened apple juice
1 can (12 ounces) orange juice concentrate,
thawed
1/2 cup water
1 tablespoon red-hot candies
1/2 teaspoon ground nutmeg
1 teaspoon whole cloves
Fresh orange slices and cinnamon sticks, optional

In a slow cooker, combine the first five ingredients. Place cloves in a double thickness of cheesecloth; bring up corners of cloth and tie with kitchen string to form a bag. Add bag to slow cooker. Cover and cook on low for 2-3 hours or until heated through. Before serving, discard spice bag and stir cider. Garnish with orange slices and cinnamon sticks if desired. **Yield:** 8 servings.

Orange Spiced Cider

Hot Reuben Spread

Hot Reuben Spread

(Pictured above)

Cook Time: 2 Hours

Rosalie Fuchs, Paynesville, Minnesota

I received the recipe for this hearty spread from my daughter. It became a fast favorite in my house.

- 1 jar (16 ounces) sauerkraut, rinsed and drained
- 1 package (8 ounces) cream cheese, cubed
- 2 cups (8 ounces) shredded Swiss cheese
- 1 package (3 ounces) deli corned beef, chopped
- 3 tablespoons Thousand Island salad dressing

Snack rye bread *or* crackers

In a 1-1/2-qt. slow cooker, combine the first five ingredients. Cover and cook for 2 hours or until cheeses are melted; stir to blend. Serve warm with bread or crackers. **Yield:** 3-1/2 cups.

Parmesan Fondue

Serve in Slow Cooker

Gwynne Fleener, Coeur d'Alene, Idaho

This rich cheese recipe was given to me at a potluck I attended on New Year's. Since then, the fondue has been a tradition at our annual open house during the holiday season.

- 1-1/2 to 2 cups milk
- 2 packages (8 ounces *each*) cream cheese, cubed
- 1-1/2 cups grated Parmesan cheese
- 1/2 teaspoon garlic salt
- 1 loaf (1 pound) French bread, cubed

In a large saucepan, cook and stir the milk and cream cheese over low heat until cheese is melted. Stir in Parmesan cheese and garlic salt; cook and stir until heated through. Transfer to a fondue pot or mini slow cooker; keep warm. Serve with bread cubes. **Yield:** about 3-1/2 cups.

Sweet-and-Sour Smokies

Cook Time: 4 Hours

Debi Hetland, Rochelle, Illinois

This warm appetizer is so simple to make but so tasty. I use cherry pie filling, chunks of pineapple and a little brown sugar to create a fruity sauce for the mini sausages.

- 2 packages (16 ounces *each*) miniature smoked sausage links
- 2 cans (21 ounces *each*) cherry pie filling
- 1 can (20 ounces) pineapple chunks, drained
- 3 tablespoons brown sugar

Place sausages in a slow cooker. In a bowl, combine the pie filling, pineapple and brown sugar; pour over sausages. Cover and cook on low for 4 hours. **Yield:** 16-20 servings.

Cranberry Meatballs

Cook Time: 6 Hours

Nina Hall, Spokane, Wisconsin

Whether you serve them as appetizers or a main course, these tasty meatballs are sure to be popular. Cranberry and chili sauces combine to give them a nice sweetness.

> 2 eggs, beaten
> 1 cup dry bread crumbs
> 1/3 cup minced fresh parsley
> 2 tablespoons finely chopped onion
> 1-1/2 pounds lean ground beef
> 1 can (16 ounces) jellied cranberry sauce
> 1 bottle (12 ounces) chili sauce
> 1/3 cup ketchup
> 2 tablespoons brown sugar
> 1 tablespoon lemon juice

In a large bowl, combine the eggs, bread crumbs, parsley and onion. Crumble beef over mixture and mix well. Shape into 1-1/2-in. balls. Place in a 3-qt. slow cooker.

In a small bowl, combine cranberry sauce, chili sauce, ketchup, brown sugar and lemon juice; mix well. Pour over the meatballs. Cover and cook on low for 6 hours or until the meat is no longer pink. **Yield:** 6 servings.

Mulled Dr. Pepper

(Pictured below)

Cook Time: 2 Hours

Bernice Morris, Marshfield, Missouri

When friends visit us on chilly evenings, I'll serve this warm beverage with ham sandwiches and deviled eggs.

> 8 cups Dr. Pepper
> 1/4 cup packed brown sugar

Mulled Dr. Pepper

Hot Crab Spread

> 1/4 cup lemon juice
> 1/2 teaspoon ground allspice
> 1/2 teaspoon whole cloves
> 1/4 teaspoon salt
> 1/4 teaspoon ground nutmeg
> 3 cinnamon sticks (3 inches)

In a 3-qt. slow cooker, combine all ingredients; mix well. Cover and cook on low for 2 hours or until desired temperature is reached. Discard cloves and cinnamon sticks before serving. **Yield:** 8-10 servings.

Hot Crab Spread

(Pictured above)

Cook Time: 1-1/2 Hours

Christine Woody, Cottage Grove, Oregon

After my mother and sister described the hot crab sandwiches they ate at a San Francisco restaurant, I developed this recipe. It's become a family favorite.

> 1-1/2 cups chopped green onions
> 6 garlic cloves, minced
> 1 tablespoon butter
> 1 tablespoon mayonnaise
> 8 cups (32 ounces) shredded Monterey Jack cheese
> 4 cans (6 ounces *each*) crabmeat, drained, flaked and cartilage removed
> Assorted crackers

In a skillet, saute onions and garlic in butter until tender. Transfer to a 3-qt. slow cooker; add mayonnaise. Stir in cheese. Cover and cook on low for 30 minutes or until cheese is melted, stirring occasionally. Stir in crab; cover and cook 1 hour longer or until heated through. Serve spread warm with crackers. **Yield:** 6 cups.

Editor's Note: Reduced-fat or fat-free mayonnaise may not be substituted for regular mayonnaise in this recipe.

Tropical Tea

In a 1-1/2-qt. slow cooker, combine the cheese sauce and soup. Cover and cook on low for 30 minutes or until cheese is melted, stirring occasionally. Stir in the broccoli, mushrooms and jalapeno. Cover and cook on low for 2 hours or until heated through. Serve with vegetables. **Yield:** 5-1/2 cups.

Editor's Note: When cutting or seeding hot peppers, use rubber or plastic gloves to protect your hands. Avoid touching your face.

Barbecue Chicken Wings

(Pictured below)

Cook Time: 1 Hour

Jean Ann Herritt, Canton, Ohio

Make sure everyone has extra napkins…these lip-smacking wings are messy to eat but oh, so good!

> 3 **pounds whole chicken wings**
> 2 **cups ketchup**
> 1/2 **cup honey**
> 2 **tablespoons lemon juice**
> 2 **tablespoons vegetable oil**
> 2 **tablespoons soy sauce**
> 2 **tablespoons Worcestershire sauce**
> 1 **tablespoon paprika**
> 4 **garlic cloves, minced**
> 1-1/2 **teaspoons curry powder**
> 1/2 **teaspoon pepper**
> 1/8 **teaspoon hot pepper sauce**

Cut chicken wings into three sections and discard wing tips. Place wings in a greased 15-in. x 10-in. x 1-in. baking pan. Bake at 350° for 35-40 minutes or until juices run clear.

In a bowl, combine the remaining ingredients. Pour 1/2 cup into a 3-qt. slow cooker. Drain chicken wings; add to slow cooker. Drizzle with remaining sauce. Cover and cook on low for 1 hour, basting occasionally. **Yield:** 10 servings.

Editor's Note: Three pounds of uncooked chicken wing sections (wingettes) may be substituted for the whole chicken wings. Omit the first step.

Tropical Tea

(Pictured above)

Cook Time: 2 to 4 Hours

Irene Helen Zundel, Carmichaels, Pennsylvania

I often brew a batch of this fragrant, flavorful tea in my slow cooker for family gatherings and parties.

> 6 **cups boiling water**
> 6 **individual tea bags**
> 1-1/2 **cups orange juice**
> 1-1/2 **cups unsweetened pineapple juice**
> 1/3 **cup sugar**
> 1 **medium navel orange, sliced and halved**
> 2 **tablespoons honey**

In a 5-qt. slow cooker, combine boiling water and tea bags. Cover and let stand for 5 minutes. Discard tea bags. Stir in the remaining ingredients. Cover and cook on low for 2-4 hours or until heated through. Serve warm. **Yield:** about 2-1/2 quarts.

Warm Broccoli Cheese Dip

Cook Time: 2-1/2 Hours

Barbara Maiol, Conyers, Georgia

This change-of-pace vegetable dip gets its flair from jalapeno pepper, mushrooms and crunchy broccoli.

> 2 **jars (8 ounces** *each***) process cheese sauce**
> 1 **can (10-3/4 ounces) condensed cream of chicken soup, undiluted**
> 1 **package (10 ounces) frozen chopped broccoli, thawed and drained**
> 1/2 **pound fresh mushrooms, chopped**
> 2 **tablespoons chopped seeded jalapeno pepper**
> **Assorted fresh vegetables**

Barbecue Chicken Wings

Warm Christmas Punch

(Pictured at right)

Cook Time: 2 to 5 Hours

Julie Sterchi, Harrisburg, Illinois

Red-hot candies add rich color and flavor to this festive punch. The cranberry juice gives it a delicious tang.

    1 bottle (32 ounces) cranberry juice
    1 can (32 ounces) pineapple juice
    1/3 cup red-hot candies
    1 cinnamon stick (3-1/2 inches)
Additional cinnamon sticks, optional

In a slow cooker, combine juices, red-hots and cinnamon stick. Cook on low for 2-5 hours. Remove cinnamon stick before serving. Use additional cinnamon sticks as stirrers if desired. **Yield:** 2 quarts.

Spiced Tea Mix

Cook Time: 4 Hours

Deb McKinney, Cedar Falls, Iowa

For years, I've relied on this homespun mix to make a hot spiced tea and a heartwarming punch.

    1 jar (21.1 ounces) orange breakfast drink mix
    1 jar (6 ounces) sugar-free instant lemon iced
       tea mix
    2/3 cup sweetened lemonade drink mix
    2 teaspoons ground cinnamon
    1 teaspoon ground cloves
ADDITIONAL INGREDIENT FOR HOT SPICED TEA:
    1 cup boiling water
ADDITIONAL INGREDIENTS FOR HOT SPICED
PUNCH:
    2 quarts apple juice *or* cider
1-1/2 cups cranberry juice
    3 cinnamon sticks (3-1/2 inches)

In an airtight container, combine the first five ingredients. Store in a cool, dry place for up to 6 months. **Yield:** about 7-1/2 cups total.

To prepare tea: Dissolve about 1 tablespoon tea mix in boiling water; stir well. **Yield:** 1 serving.

To prepare punch: In a slow cooker, combine the juices, 1/4 to 1/3 cup tea mix and cinnamon sticks. Cover and cook on low for 4 hours. **Yield:** about 12 servings (6 ounces each).

Sweet 'n' Spicy Meatballs

Serve in Slow Cooker

Genie Brown, Roanoke, Virginia

You'll usually find a batch of these meatballs in my freezer. The slightly sweet sauce complements the spicy sausage.

Warm Christmas Punch

    2 pounds bulk hot pork sausage
    1 egg, lightly beaten
    1 cup packed brown sugar
    1 cup red wine vinegar
    1 cup ketchup
    1 tablespoon soy sauce
    1 teaspoon ground ginger

In a large bowl, combine the sausage and egg. Shape into 1-in. balls. Place in a greased 15-in. x 10-in. x 1-in. baking pan. Bake at 400° for 15-20 minutes or until meat is no longer pink. Meanwhile, in a saucepan, combine the brown sugar, vinegar, ketchup, soy sauce and ginger. Bring to a boil. Reduce heat; simmer, uncovered, until sugar is dissolved.

Transfer meatballs to a 3-qt. slow cooker. Add the sauce and stir gently to coat. Cover and keep warm on low until serving. **Yield:** about 4 dozen.

Meaty Chili Dip

Serve in Slow Cooker

Karen Kiel, Camdenton, Missouri

A meaty snack like this is a must for the men in my family. They eat it with corn chips and scrape the bowl clean!

    1 pound ground beef
    1 medium green pepper, chopped
    1 cup water
    1 can (6 ounces) tomato paste
    1 package (3 ounces) cream cheese, cubed
    1 envelope chili seasoning mix
Corn chips

In a large skillet, cook beef and green pepper over medium heat until meat is no longer pink; drain. Add the water, tomato paste, cream cheese and chili seasoning mix. Bring to a boil. Reduce heat; simmer, uncovered, until cheese is melted. Transfer to a small slow cooker to keep warm. Serve with corn chips. **Yield:** 3 cups.

Soups & Sandwiches

French Dip (p. 29)

Chapter 2

Tangy Bean Soup

Tangy Bean Soup

(Pictured above)

Cook Time: 4-1/2 to 5-1/2 Hours

Joan Hallford, North Richland Hills, Texas

This soup has a great southwestern flavor and is a real winner with my family. I can quickly make the dumplings just before mealtime, and dinner's done in a jiffy.

> 2 cans (14-1/2 ounces *each*) chicken broth
> 1 package (16 ounces) frozen mixed vegetables
> 1 can (15 ounces) black beans, rinsed and drained
> 1 can (15 ounces) pinto beans, rinsed and drained
> 1 can (14-1/2 ounces) diced tomatoes, undrained
> 1 medium onion, chopped
> 1 tablespoon chili powder
> 1 tablespoon minced fresh cilantro
> 4 garlic cloves, minced
> 1/4 teaspoon pepper

CORNMEAL DUMPLINGS:
> 1/2 cup all-purpose flour
> 1/2 cup shredded sharp cheddar cheese
> 1/3 cup cornmeal
> 1 tablespoon sugar
> 1 teaspoon baking powder
> 1 egg
> 2 tablespoons milk
> 2 teaspoons vegetable oil

In a slow cooker, combine the first 10 ingredients. Cover and cook on high for 4-5 hours.

For dumplings, combine the flour, cheese, cornmeal, sugar and baking powder in a bowl. In anoth-er bowl, combine the egg, milk and oil; add to dry ingredients just until moistened (batter will be stiff). Drop by heaping tablespoons onto soup. Cover and cook on high 30 minutes longer (without lifting the cover) or until a toothpick inserted in a dumpling comes out clean. **Yield:** 6 servings.

Brats with Sauerkraut

(Pictured below)

Cook Time: 6 to 7 Hours

Darlene Dixon, Hanover, Minnesota

I've made many variations of this excellent main dish. The bratwurst can be plain, smoked or cheese-flavored, served whole or cut in slices, eaten with a bun or without.

> 8 uncooked bratwurst
> 1 can (14 ounces) sauerkraut, rinsed and well drained
> 2 medium apples, peeled and finely chopped
> 3 bacon strips, cooked and crumbled
> 1/4 cup packed brown sugar
> 1/4 cup finely chopped onion
> 1 teaspoon ground mustard
> 8 bratwurst buns, split

Place bratwurst in a 5-qt. slow cooker. In a large bowl, combine the sauerkraut, apples, bacon, brown sugar, onion and mustard; spoon over bratwurst. Cover and cook on low for 6-7 hours or until sausage is no longer pink. Place bratwurst in buns; using a slotted spoon, top with the sauerkraut mixture. **Yield:** 8 servings.

Brats with Sauerkraut

Soups & Sandwiches

Mexican Chicken Soup

(Pictured at right)

Cook Time: 3 to 4 Hours

Marlene Kane, Lainesburg, Michigan

This zesty dish is loaded with chicken, corn and black beans. We love the taco-like taste in every spoonful.

1-1/2 pounds boneless skinless chicken breasts, cubed
2 teaspoons canola oil
1/2 cup water
1 envelope taco seasoning
1 can (32 ounces) V8 juice
1 jar (16 ounces) salsa
1 can (15 ounces) black beans, rinsed and drained
1 package (10 ounces) frozen corn, thawed
6 tablespoons cheddar cheese
6 tablespoons sour cream
2 tablespoons chopped fresh cilantro *or* parsley

In a large nonstick skillet, saute chicken in oil until no longer pink. Add water and taco seasoning; simmer until chicken is well coated. Transfer to a slow cooker. Add V8 juice, salsa, beans and corn; mix well. Cover and cook on low for 3-4 hours or until heated through. Serve with cheese, sour cream and cilantro. **Yield:** 6 servings.

Mexican Chicken Soup

Slow-Cooked Chowder

Cook Time: 6 to 7 Hours

Pam Leonard, Aberdeen, South Dakota

The hectic holiday season often leaves little time for cooking. That's why this fix-it-and-forget-it recipe is one of my favorites at Christmastime. The chowder requires little prep work before you put it in the slow cooker, and the taste is wonderful.

5 cups water
5 teaspoons chicken bouillon granules
8 medium potatoes, cubed
2 medium onions, chopped
1 medium carrot, thinly sliced
1 celery rib, thinly sliced
1/4 cup butter, cubed
1 teaspoon salt
1/4 teaspoon pepper
1 can (12 ounces) evaporated milk
1 tablespoon minced fresh parsley

In a 5-qt. slow cooker, combine the first nine ingredients. Cover and cook on high for 1 hour. Reduce the heat to low; cover and cook for 5-6 hours or until the vegetables are tender. Stir in the evaporated milk and parsley; heat through. **Yield:** 12 servings (about 3 quarts).

Ham and Lentil Soup

Cook Time: 4 Hours

Connie Jones Pixley, Roxboro, North Carolina

Lentil lovers can't resist this satisfying soup. Pop it in the slow cooker after lunch, and it'll be ready by suppertime.

1 cup chopped celery
1 cup chopped carrots
1/2 cup chopped onion
1 tablespoon butter
8 cups water
2 cups dried lentils, rinsed
1 cup cubed fully cooked ham
2 teaspoons salt
1 teaspoon dried marjoram
1/2 teaspoon pepper

In a large skillet, saute the celery, carrots and onion in butter for 3-4 minutes or until crisp-tender. In a 5-qt. slow cooker, combine the water, lentils, ham, salt, marjoram and pepper. Stir in the celery mixture. Cover and cook on low for 4 hours or until lentils are tender. **Yield:** 11 servings.

Give Soup a Great Garnish

Adding a garnish to soup before serving gives color and adds to the flavor and texture. Easy ideas include: finely chopped green onions or chives, minced fresh parsley, shredded cheddar cheese, grated or shredded Parmesan cheese, a dollop of sour cream and plain or seasoned croutons.

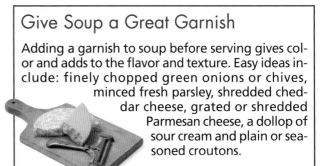

Hearty Split Pea Soup

Cook Time: 4 to 5 Hours

Deanna Waggy, South Bend, Indiana

This tasty soup is one of my favorite meals to make during the workweek. When I get home, I just add the milk.

- 1 package (16 ounces) dried split peas
- 2 cups diced fully cooked lean ham
- 1 cup diced carrots
- 1 medium onion, chopped
- 2 garlic cloves, minced
- 2 bay leaves
- 1/2 teaspoon salt
- 1/2 teaspoon pepper
- 5 cups boiling water
- 1 cup hot milk

In a slow cooker, layer the first nine ingredients in the order listed (do not stir). Cover and cook on high for 4-5 hours or until the vegetables are tender. Stir in the milk. Discard the bay leaves before serving. **Yield:** 9 servings.

Bandito Chili Dogs

(Pictured below)

Cook Time: 4 to 5 Hours

Marion Lowery, Medford, Oregon

These beefy dogs can cook while you're at a sports event or other activity, so the meal is ready when you get home.

- 1 package (1 pound) hot dogs
- 2 cans (15 ounces *each*) chili without beans
- 1 can (10-3/4 ounces) condensed cheddar cheese soup, undiluted
- 1 can (4 ounces) chopped green chilies
- 10 hot dog buns, split
- 1 medium onion, chopped
- 1 to 2 cups corn chips, coarsely crushed
- 1 cup (4 ounces) shredded cheddar cheese

Place hot dogs in a slow cooker. In a bowl, combine the chili, soup and green chilies; pour over hot dogs. Cover and cook on low for 4-5 hours. Serve hot dogs in buns; top with chili mixture, onion, corn chips and cheese. **Yield:** 10 servings.

Minestrone Soup

(Pictured above right)

Cook Time: 7 to 9 Hours

Kara de la Vega, Somerset, California

When this hearty minestrone has 30 minutes left to cook, I just add the macaroni and slice some French bread.

- 6 cups chicken broth
- 1 can (15 ounces) garbanzo beans *or* chickpeas, rinsed and drained
- 1 medium potato, peeled and cubed
- 1 cup cubed deli ham
- 1/3 cup chopped onion
- 1 small carrot, chopped
- 1 celery rib, chopped

Bandito Chili Dogs

Minestrone Soup

In a small skillet, saute onion in butter until tender. In a 5-qt. slow cooker, combine the onion mixture, milk, soups, corn, Creole seasoning and garlic powder. Cover and cook on low for 3 hours. Stir in shrimp and cream cheese.

Cook 30 minutes longer or until shrimp are heated through and cheese is melted. Stir to blend. Garnish with bacon. **Yield:** 12 servings (3 quarts).

Slow-Cooked Potato Soup

(Pictured below)

Cook Time: 5 to 6 Hours

Mary Jo O'Brien, Hastings, Minnesota

I make this thick, creamy soup for our annual St. Patrick's Day party, and there's never any left.

- 5-1/2 cups cubed peeled potatoes, divided
- 2-3/4 cups water
- 1/3 cup butter, cubed
- 1-1/3 cups cubed fully cooked ham
- 2 celery ribs, chopped
- 2/3 cup chopped onion
- 3/4 teaspoon garlic powder
- 3/4 teaspoon paprika
- 1/8 teaspoon pepper
- 1/2 pound process cheese (Velveeta), cubed
- 2/3 cup sour cream
- Milk, optional

Place 4-1/2 cups of the potatoes in a saucepan; add water. Bring to a boil. Reduce heat; cover and cook for 15-20 minutes or until tender. Remove from heat (do not drain). Mash potatoes; stir in butter.

In a 3-qt. slow cooker, combine the ham, celery, onion, garlic powder, paprika, pepper and remaining cubed potatoes. Stir in the mashed potatoes; top with cheese. Cover and cook on low for 5-6 hours or until potatoes and other vegetables are tender. Stir in the sour cream until blended. Thin soup with milk if desired. **Yield:** 6 servings.

- 2 tablespoons minced fresh parsley
- 1/2 teaspoon minced garlic
- 1/2 cup uncooked elbow macaroni
- 1 can (14-1/2 ounces) diced tomatoes, undrained
- 1 package (10 ounces) frozen chopped spinach, thawed and squeezed dry

In a 5-qt. slow cooker, combine the first nine ingredients. Cover and cook on high for 1 hour. Reduce heat to low; cook for 6-8 hours or until vegetables are almost tender.

During the last 30 minutes of cooking, stir in the macaroni. Cover and cook until macaroni is tender. Stir in the tomatoes and spinach; heat through. **Yield:** 10 servings.

Shrimp Chowder

Cook Time: 3-1/2 Hours

Will Zunio, Gretna, Louisiana

Because this chowder is ready in less than 4 hours, it can be prepared in the afternoon and served that night.

- 1/2 cup chopped onion
- 2 teaspoons butter
- 2 cans (12 ounces *each*) evaporated milk
- 2 cans (10-3/4 ounces *each*) condensed cream of potato soup, undiluted
- 2 cans (10-3/4 ounces *each*) condensed cream of chicken soup, undiluted
- 1 can (11 ounces) white *or* shoepeg corn, drained
- 1 teaspoon Creole seasoning
- 1/2 teaspoon garlic powder
- 2 pounds cooked small shrimp, peeled and deveined
- 1 package (3 ounces) cream cheese, cubed
- 4 bacon strips, cooked and crumbled

Slow-Cooked Potato Soup

Spicy Kielbasa Soup

Spicy Kielbasa Soup

(Pictured above)

Cook Time: 8 to 9 Hours

Carol Custer, Clifton Park, New York

Red pepper flakes bring a little zip to this hearty soup that's full of good-for-you ingredients. Should you have any left over, the soup is great reheated.

- 1/2 pound smoked turkey kielbasa, sliced
- 1 medium onion, chopped
- 1 medium green pepper, chopped
- 1 celery rib with leaves, thinly sliced
- 4 garlic cloves, minced
- 2 cans (14-1/2 ounces *each*) reduced-sodium chicken broth
- 1 can (15-1/2 ounces) great northern beans, rinsed and drained
- 1 can (14-1/2 ounces) stewed tomatoes, cut up
- 1 small zucchini, sliced
- 1 medium carrot, shredded
- 1 tablespoon dried parsley flakes
- 1/4 teaspoon crushed red pepper flakes
- 1/4 teaspoon pepper

In a nonstick skillet, cook kielbasa over medium heat until lightly browned. Add the onion, green pepper, celery and garlic. Cook and stir for 5 minutes or until vegetables are tender. Transfer to a slow cooker. Stir in the remaining ingredients. Cover and cook on low for 8-9 hours. **Yield:** 5 servings.

Shredded Steak Sandwiches

(Pictured below)

Cook Time: 6 to 8 Hours

Lee Deneau, Lansing, Michigan

This saucy steak barbecue makes a quick meal served on buns or even over rice, potatoes or buttered noodles.

- 3 pounds boneless beef round steak, cut into large pieces
- 2 large onions, chopped
- 3/4 cup thinly sliced celery
- 1-1/2 cups ketchup
- 1/2 to 3/4 cup water
- 1/3 cup lemon juice
- 1/3 cup Worcestershire sauce
- 3 tablespoons brown sugar
- 3 tablespoons cider vinegar
- 2 to 3 teaspoons salt
- 2 teaspoons prepared mustard
- 1-1/2 teaspoons paprika
- 1 teaspoon chili powder
- 1/2 teaspoon pepper
- 1/8 to 1/4 teaspoon hot pepper sauce
- 12 to 14 sandwich rolls, split

Place meat in a 5-qt. slow cooker. Add onions and celery. In a bowl, combine the ketchup, water, lemon juice, Worcestershire sauce, brown sugar, vinegar, salt, mustard, paprika, chili powder, pepper and hot pepper sauce. Pour over meat. Cover and cook on high for 6-8 hours.

Remove meat; cool slightly. Shred with a fork. Return to the sauce and heat through. Serve on rolls. **Yield:** 12-14 servings.

Shredded Steak Sandwiches

Italian Beef Sandwiches

(Pictured at right)

Cook Time: 8 to 9 Hours

Kristin Swihart, Perrysburg, Ohio

I'm a paramedic/firefighter, and slow-cooked recipes like this one suit my hectic schedule. My family and the hungry bunch at the firehouse love these robust sandwiches.

    1 jar (11-1/2 ounces) pepperoncinis
    1 boneless beef chuck roast (3-1/2 to 4
       pounds)
  1/4 cup water
1-3/4 teaspoons dried basil
1-1/2 teaspoons garlic powder
1-1/2 teaspoons dried oregano
1-1/4 teaspoons salt
  1/4 teaspoon pepper
    1 large onion, sliced and quartered
   10 to 12 hard rolls, split

Italian Beef Sandwiches

Drain pepperoncinis, reserving liquid. Remove and discard stems of peppers; set peppers aside. Cut roast into large chunks; place a third of the meat in a 5-qt. slow cooker. Add water.

In a small bowl, combine the basil, garlic powder, oregano, salt and pepper; sprinkle half over beef. Layer with half of the remaining meat, then onion, reserved peppers and liquid. Top with remaining meat and herb mixture.

Cover and cook on low for 8-9 hours or until meat is tender. Shred beef with two forks. Using a slotted spoon, serve beef and peppers on rolls. **Yield:** 10-12 servings.

Editor's Note: Look for pepperoncinis (pickled peppers) in the pickle and olive section of your grocery store.

Slow-Cooked Corn Chowder

Cook Time: 6 Hours

Mary Hogue, Rochester, Pennsylvania

I combine and refrigerate the ingredients for this easy chowder the night before. In the morning, I pour the mixture into the slow cooker and turn it on before I leave for work.

2-1/2 cups milk
    1 can (14-3/4 ounces) cream-style corn
    1 can (10-3/4 ounces) condensed cream of
       mushroom soup, undiluted
1-3/4 cups frozen corn
    1 cup frozen shredded hash brown potatoes
    1 cup cubed fully cooked ham
    1 large onion, chopped
    2 tablespoons butter
    2 teaspoons dried parsley flakes
Salt and pepper to taste

In a slow cooker, combine all ingredients. Cover and cook on low for 6 hours. **Yield:** 8 servings (2 quarts).

Slow-Cooked Pork Barbecue

Cook Time: 5 to 6 Hours

Connie Johnson, Springfield, Missouri

I need only a handful of items to fix this sweet and tender shredded pork for sandwiches. Feel free to adjust the sauce ingredients to suit your family's tastes.

    1 boneless pork loin roast (3 to 4 pounds)
1-1/2 teaspoons seasoned salt
    1 teaspoon garlic powder
    1 cup barbecue sauce
    1 cup cola
    8 to 10 sandwich rolls, split

Cut roast in half; place in a slow cooker. Sprinkle with seasoned salt and garlic powder. Cover and cook on low for 4 hours or until meat is tender.

Remove meat; skim fat from cooking juices. Shred meat with a fork and return to the slow cooker. Combine barbecue sauce and cola; pour over meat. Cover and cook on high for 1-2 hours or until sauce is thickened. Serve on rolls. **Yield:** 8-10 servings.

Fresh Pumpkin Soup

(Pictured below)

Cook Time: 8 to 10 Hours

Jane Shapton, Portland, Oregon

This appealing soup harvests the fall flavors of just-picked pumpkins and tart apples…and is sure to delight you and your family on a crisp autumn day.

        8 cups chopped fresh pumpkin
          (about 3 pounds)
        4 cups chicken broth
        3 small tart apples, peeled and chopped
        1 medium onion, chopped
        2 tablespoons lemon juice
      1/2 teaspoon ground ginger *or* 2 tablespoons
          minced fresh gingerroot
        2 garlic cloves, minced
      1/2 teaspoon salt
TOASTED PUMPKIN SEEDS:
      1/2 cup pumpkin seeds
        1 teaspoon canola oil
      1/8 teaspoon salt

In a 5-qt. slow cooker, combine the first eight ingredients; mix well. Cover and cook on low for 8-10 hours or until the pumpkin and apples are tender. Meanwhile, toss the pumpkin seeds with oil and salt. Spread in an ungreased 15-in. x 10-in. x 1-in. baking pan. Bake at 250° for 50-60 minutes or until golden brown. Set aside.

Cool pumpkin mixture slightly; process in batches in a blender or food processor. Transfer to a large saucepan; heat through. Garnish with toasted pumpkin seeds. **Yield:** 9 servings.

Fresh Pumpkin Soup

Sausage Pepper Sandwiches

Cook Time: 8 Hours

Suzette Gessel, Albuquerque, New Mexico

Peppers and onion add a fresh taste to this satisfying filling for hoagie sandwiches. My mother gave me the comforting recipe, and I've enjoyed it many times.

        5 uncooked Italian sausage links (about 20
          ounces)
        1 medium green pepper, cut into 1-inch pieces
        1 medium sweet red pepper, cut into 1-inch
          pieces
        1 large onion, cut into 1-inch pieces
        1 can (8 ounces) tomato sauce
      1/8 teaspoon pepper
        6 hoagie *or* submarine sandwich buns, split

In a large skillet, brown the Italian sausage links over medium heat. Cut into 1/2-in. slices; place in a slow cooker. Stir in the peppers, onion, tomato sauce and pepper.

Cover and cook on low for 8 hours or until the sausage is no longer pink and the vegetables are tender. Use a slotted spoon to serve on buns. **Yield:** 6 servings.

Red Bean Vegetable Soup

Cook Time: 6 Hours

Ronnie Lappe, Brownwood, Texas

The addition of Cajun seasoning boosts the flavor of this brothy soup, and the easy recipe makes a big batch.

        3 large sweet red peppers, chopped
        3 celery ribs, chopped
        2 medium onions, chopped
        4 cans (16 ounces *each*) red kidney beans,
          rinsed and drained
        4 cups chicken broth
        2 bay leaves
      1/2 to 1 teaspoon salt
      1/2 to 1 teaspoon Cajun seasoning
      1/2 teaspoon pepper
      1/4 to 1/2 teaspoon hot pepper sauce

In a 5-qt. slow cooker, combine the peppers, celery, onions and beans. Stir in the remaining ingredients. Cover and cook on low for 6 hours or until vegetables are tender. Discard the bay leaves before serving. **Yield:** 12 servings (3 quarts).

Hearty Chicken Noodle Soup

Hearty Chicken Noodle Soup

(Pictured above)

Cook Time: 5-1/2 to 6-1/2 Hours

Norma Reynolds, Overland Park, Kansas

This homemade soup with a hint of cayenne is chock-full of vegetables, chicken and noodles. I revised a recipe from my father-in-law to come up with this version.

- 12 fresh baby carrots, cut into 1/2-inch pieces
- 4 celery ribs, cut into 1/2-inch pieces
- 3/4 cup finely chopped onion
- 1 tablespoon minced fresh parsley
- 1/2 teaspoon pepper
- 1/4 teaspoon cayenne pepper
- 1-1/2 teaspoons mustard seed
- 2 garlic cloves, peeled and halved
- 1-1/4 pounds boneless skinless chicken breast halves
- 1-1/4 pounds boneless skinless chicken thighs
- 4 cans (14-1/2 ounces *each*) chicken broth
- 1 package (9 ounces) refrigerated linguine

In a 5-qt. slow cooker, combine the first six ingredients. Place mustard seed and garlic on a double thickness of cheesecloth; bring up corners of cloth and tie with kitchen string to form a bag. Place in slow cooker. Add chicken and broth. Cover and cook on low for 5-6 hours or until chicken juices run clear.

Discard the spice bag. Remove the chicken; cool slightly. Stir the linguine into the soup; cover and cook for 30 minutes or until tender. Cut chicken into pieces and return to soup; heat through. **Yield: 12 servings (3 quarts).**

Mitten Sandwiches

(Pictured below)

Cook Time: 8 Hours

Charm Holman, Springfield, Missouri

Although you don't wear them, these cute mitten-shaped sandwiches are sure to warm you up. Frozen bread dough is formed into mitten buns, then filled with slow-cooked beef.

- 1 boneless beef chuck roast (about 2 pounds)
- 1 loaf (1 pound) frozen bread dough, thawed
- Red liquid food coloring
- 1 egg
- 1 tablespoon water
- 1 cup barbecue sauce
- 1/2 cup packed brown sugar
- 1/2 cup ketchup
- 1/2 cup grape jelly

Place the roast in a slow cooker. Cover and cook on low for 8 hours or until the meat is tender.

Meanwhile, divide bread dough into eighths. Tint two portions with red food coloring; divide red portions into thirds. Roll each into a 3-in. rope; set aside. For each mitten, flatten one white portion into a 4-in. oval. Place on a greased baking sheet. With a sharp knife or kitchen shears, make a 1-1/2-in. diagonal cut into side of oval toward the center for the thumb. Tuck tip under to form a round thumb; spread thumb and mitten apart.

For cuff of mitten, place a colored rope below each mitten; pinch the edges together and flatten slightly. In a small bowl, beat egg and water; brush over dough (dough does not need to rise). Bake at 350° for 15-20 minutes or until golden brown. Cool on a wire rack.

Remove roast from slow cooker; discard juices. Shred beef with a fork and return to slow cooker. Add the barbecue sauce, brown sugar, ketchup and jelly; heat through. Split mitten rolls; fill with shredded beef. **Yield: 6 sandwiches.**

Mitten Sandwiches

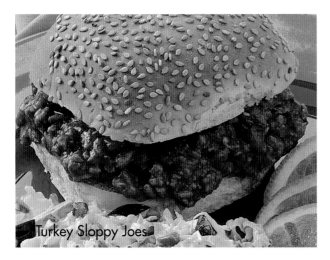

Turkey Sloppy Joes

Turkey Sloppy Joes

(Pictured above)

Cook Time: 4 Hours

Marylou LaRue, Freeland, Michigan

This tangy sandwich filling is so easy to prepare in the slow cooker, and it goes over well at large and small gatherings.

    1 pound ground turkey breast
    1 small onion, chopped
    1/2 cup chopped celery
    1/4 cup chopped green pepper
    1 can (10-3/4 ounces) condensed tomato soup, undiluted
    1/2 cup ketchup
    1 tablespoon brown sugar
    2 tablespoons prepared mustard
    1/4 teaspoon pepper
    8 hamburger buns, split

In a large saucepan coated with nonstick cooking spray, cook the turkey, onion, celery and green pepper over medium heat until meat is no longer pink; drain if necessary. Stir in the soup, ketchup, brown sugar, mustard and pepper. Transfer to a slow cooker. Cover and cook on low for 4 hours. Serve on buns. **Yield:** 8 servings.

Beef Barley Lentil Soup

Cook Time: 8 Hours

Judy Metzentine, The Dalles, Oregon

It's easy for me to fill up my slow cooker and forget about supper…until the kitchen is filled with a wonderful aroma, that is! I've served this soup often on cold nights, along with oven-fresh rolls and a green salad.

    1 pound lean ground beef
    1 medium onion, chopped
    2 cups cubed red potatoes (1/4-inch pieces)
    1 cup chopped celery
    1 cup diced carrots
    1 cup dried lentils, rinsed
    1/2 cup medium pearl barley
    8 cups water
    2 teaspoons beef bouillon granules
    1 teaspoon salt
    1/2 teaspoon lemon-pepper seasoning
    2 cans (14-1/2 ounces *each*) stewed tomatoes

In a nonstick skillet, cook beef and onion over medium heat until meat is no longer pink; drain. Transfer to a 5-qt. slow cooker. Layer with the potatoes, celery, carrots, lentils and barley. Combine the water, bouillon, salt and lemon-pepper; pour over vegetables. Cover and cook on low for 6 hours or until vegetables and barley are tender. Add the tomatoes; cook 2 hours longer. **Yield:** 10 servings.

Italian Sausage Hoagies

(Pictured below)

Cook Time: 4 Hours

Craig Wachs, Racine, Wisconsin

Our cuisine is influenced by both Germans and Italians who immigrated to this area. When preparing this recipe, we often substitute German bratwurst for the Italian sausage.

    10 uncooked Italian sausage links
    2 tablespoons olive oil
    1 jar (26 ounces) meatless spaghetti sauce
    1/2 medium green pepper, julienned
    1/2 medium sweet red pepper, julienned
    1/2 cup water
    1/4 cup grated Romano cheese
    2 tablespoons dried oregano
    2 tablespoons dried basil
    2 loaves French bread (20 inches *each*)

In a large skillet over medium-high heat, brown sausage in oil; drain. Transfer to a 5-qt. slow cooker. Add the spaghetti sauce, peppers, water, cheese, oregano and basil. Cover and cook on low for 4 hours or until sausage is no longer pink.

Italian Sausage Hoagies

Slice both loaves of French bread lengthwise but not all of the way through; cut each widthwise into five pieces. Fill each with sausage, peppers and sauce. **Yield:** 10 servings.

Savory Winter Soup

(Pictured at right)

Cook Time: 8 Hours

Dana Simmons, Lancaster, Ohio

Even my father, who doesn't particularly like soup, enjoys my full-flavored version of traditional vegetable soup. It's a delightful meal after a long day.

- 2 **pounds ground beef**
- 3 **medium onions, chopped**
- 1 **garlic clove, minced**
- 3 **cans (10-1/2 ounces** *each*) **condensed beef broth, undiluted**
- 1 **can (28 ounces) diced tomatoes, undrained**
- 3 **cups water**
- 1 **cup** *each* **diced carrots and celery**
- 1 **cup fresh** *or* **frozen cut green beans**
- 1 **cup cubed peeled potatoes**
- 2 **tablespoons minced fresh parsley** *or* 2 **teaspoons dried parsley flakes**
- 1 **teaspoon dried basil**
- 1/2 **teaspoon dried thyme**

Salt and pepper to taste

In a skillet, cook beef, onions and garlic over medium heat until the meat is no longer pink; drain. Transfer to a 5-qt. slow cooker. Add the remaining ingredients and mix well. Cover and cook on high for 8 hours or until heated through. **Yield:** 14 servings (3-1/2 quarts).

Cheese Soup for Two

Cook Time: 6 Hours

Ann Huseby, Lakeville, Minnesota

This comforting soup for a pair is a welcome treat on wintry days. Garnish it with croutons, bacon or onions.

- 1 **can (14-1/2 ounces) chicken broth**
- 1/4 **cup chopped carrot**
- 1/4 **cup chopped celery**
- 1 **tablespoon chopped onion**
- 1 **tablespoon chopped sweet red pepper**
- 2 **teaspoons butter**
- 1/8 **to 1/4 teaspoon pepper**
- 2 **tablespoons all-purpose flour**
- 2 **tablespoons cold water**
- 1 **package (3 ounces) cream cheese, cubed and softened**
- 3/4 **cup shredded cheddar cheese**
- 1/3 **cup beer** *or* **additional chicken broth**

Savory Winter Soup

Croutons, crumbled cooked bacon and sliced green onions, optional

In a 1-1/2 qt. slow cooker, combine the first seven ingredients. Cover and cook on low for 5 hours.

Combine the flour and water until smooth; stir into soup. Cover and cook on high for 30 minutes or until thickened.

Stir in cream cheese and cheddar cheese until blended. Stir in beer or additional broth. Cover and cook on low for 10 minutes or until heated through. Top with croutons, bacon and green onions if desired. **Yield:** 2 servings.

Chicken Vegetable Soup

Cook Time: 6 to 8 Hours

Connie Thomas, Jensen, Utah

This specialty tastes great, comes together easily and is nutritious, too. It's one of my favorite recipes.

- 1 **can (28 ounces) diced tomatoes, undrained**
- 2 **cups chicken broth**
- 2 **cups cubed cooked chicken breast**
- 1 **cup frozen corn**
- 2 **celery ribs with leaves, chopped**
- 1 **can (6 ounces) tomato paste**
- 1/4 **cup dried lentils, rinsed**
- 1 **tablespoon sugar**
- 1 **tablespoon Worcestershire sauce**
- 2 **teaspoons dried parsley flakes**
- 1 **teaspoon dried marjoram**

In a slow cooker, combine all ingredients. Cover and cook on low for 6-8 hours or until vegetables are tender. **Yield:** 8 servings (2 quarts).

Chicken Soup with Beans

(Pictured below)

Cook Time: 6 to 7 Hours

Penny Peronia, West Memphis, Arkansas

I put lime-flavored tortilla chips at the bottom of individual bowls before ladling in this southwestern soup.

  1 large onion, chopped
  2 garlic cloves, minced
  1 tablespoon vegetable oil
1-1/4 pounds boneless skinless chicken breasts, cooked and cubed
  2 cans (15-1/2 ounces *each*) great northern beans, rinsed and drained
  2 cans (11 ounces *each*) white *or* shoepeg corn, drained
  1 can (10 ounces) diced tomatoes and green chilies, undrained
  3 cups water
  1 can (4 ounces) chopped green chilies
  2 tablespoons lime juice
  1 teaspoon lemon-pepper seasoning
  1 teaspoon ground cumin
 1/4 teaspoon salt
 1/4 teaspoon pepper

In a skillet, saute onion and garlic in oil until tender. Transfer to a 5-qt. slow cooker. Stir in the chicken, beans, corn, tomatoes, water, chopped green chilies, lime juice and seasonings. Cover and cook on low for 6-7 hours or until heated through. **Yield:** 12 servings (3 quarts).

Chicken Soup with Beans

Brisket for a Bunch

Brisket for a Bunch

(Pictured above)

Cook Time: 7 to 8 Hours

Dawn Fagerstrom, Warren, Minnesota

This recipe simmers slices of beef in a wonderfully savory au jus.

  1 beef brisket (2-1/2 pounds), cut in half
  1 tablespoon vegetable oil
1/2 cup chopped celery
1/2 cup chopped onion
3/4 cup beef broth
1/2 cup tomato sauce
1/4 cup water
1/4 cup sugar
  2 tablespoons onion soup mix
  1 tablespoon vinegar
12 hamburger buns, split

In a large skillet, brown the brisket on all sides in oil; transfer to a slow cooker. In the same skillet, saute celery and onion for 1 minute. Gradually add broth, tomato sauce and water; stir to loosen the browned bits from pan. Add sugar, soup mix and vinegar; bring to a boil. Pour over brisket.

Cover and cook on low for 7-8 hours or until meat is tender. Let stand for 5 minutes before slicing. Skim fat from cooking juices. Serve meat in buns with cooking juices. **Yield:** 12 servings.

Editor's Note: This recipe is for fresh beef brisket, not corned beef.

Hearty Goose Soup

Cook Time: 5 Hours

Loretta Fenrich, Barney Lake, Washington

After my son went goose hunting, I had to find recipes upon his return. I came up with this chunky soup.

- 2-1/4 cups cubed uncooked goose
- 1 pound red potatoes, cubed
- 1 large onion, chopped
- 1 *each* medium green, sweet yellow and red pepper, chopped
- 2 medium carrots, cut into 1/2-inch slices
- 1 cup water
- 3 garlic cloves, minced
- 2 teaspoons dried basil
- Salt and pepper to taste
- 1 can (15 ounces) tomato sauce
- 1 can (14-1/2 ounces) Italian stewed tomatoes
- 2 cups uncooked elbow macaroni

In a 5-qt. slow cooker, combine goose, potatoes, onion, peppers, carrots, water, garlic, basil, salt and pepper. Cover and cook on high for 4 hours or until meat juices run clear and vegetables are tender.

Stir in tomato sauce and tomatoes; cook 1 hour longer. Just before serving, cook macaroni according to package directions; drain. Stir into the soup. **Yield:** 13 servings (about 3 quarts).

Shredded Venison Sandwiches

Cook Time: 4-1/2 to 5 Hours

Ruth Setterlund, Freyburg, Maine

My husband hunts for deer every November, so I'm always looking for new recipes for venison. The whole family loves these well-seasoned sandwiches.

- 1 boneless venison roast (4 pounds)
- 1-1/2 cups ketchup
- 3 tablespoons brown sugar
- 1 tablespoon ground mustard
- 1 tablespoon lemon juice
- 1 tablespoon soy sauce
- 1 tablespoon Liquid Smoke, optional
- 2 teaspoons celery salt
- 2 teaspoons pepper
- 2 teaspoons Worcestershire sauce
- 1 teaspoon onion powder
- 1 teaspoon garlic powder
- 1/8 teaspoon ground nutmeg
- 3 drops hot pepper sauce
- 14 to 18 hamburger buns, split

Cut venison roast in half; place in a 5-qt. slow cooker. In a large bowl, combine the ketchup, brown sugar, mustard, lemon juice, soy sauce, Liquid Smoke if desired and seasonings. Pour Cover and cook on high for 4-1/2 to til meat is tender.

Remove the roast; set aside to cool and return to slow cooker. Shred mea forks; stir into sauce and heat through. ted spoon, spoon meat mixture onto bun. **Yield:** 14-18 servings.

French Dip

(Pictured below and on page 16)

Cook Time: 5 to 6 Hours

Margaret McNeil, Memphis, Tennessee

For a sandwich with more pizzazz than the traditional French dip, give this recipe a try. The seasonings give the broth a great flavor, and the meat cooks up tender and juicy.

- 1 beef chuck roast (3 pounds), trimmed
- 2 cups water
- 1/2 cup soy sauce
- 1 teaspoon dried rosemary
- 1 teaspoon dried thyme
- 1 teaspoon garlic powder
- 1 bay leaf
- 3 to 4 whole peppercorns
- 8 French rolls, split

Place roast in a slow cooker. Add water, soy sauce and seasonings. Cover and cook on high for 5-6 hours or until beef is tender. Remove meat from broth; shred with forks and keep warm. Strain broth; skim off fat. Pour broth into small cups for dipping. Serve beef on rolls. **Yield:** 8 servings.

French Dip

Teriyaki Pulled Pork Sandwiches

Teriyaki Pulled Pork Sandwiches

(Pictured above)

Cook Time: 7-1/2 to 8-1/2 Hours

With this recipe from our Test Kitchen, you'll discover how nice it is to come home to the aroma of pork roast simmering in pineapple juice and teriyaki sauce. Add these sandwiches to your workweek lineup, and no one will be disappointed.

- 1 boneless pork shoulder roast (3 pounds), trimmed
- 2 teaspoons olive oil
- 1 cup finely chopped onion
- 1 cup teriyaki sauce, *divided*
- 1/2 cup unsweetened pineapple juice
- 3 tablespoons all-purpose flour
- 8 whole wheat hamburger buns, split
- 1 can (20 ounces) sliced pineapple, drained

In a large skillet, brown roast in oil over medium-high heat. Cut the roast in half; place in a 5-qt. slow cooker. Add the onion, 1/2 cup teriyaki sauce and pineapple juice. Cover and cook on low for 7-8 hours or until meat is tender.

Remove roast; set aside. In a small bowl, combine the flour and remaining teriyaki sauce until smooth; stir into cooking juices. Cover and cook on high for 30-40 minutes or until thickened.

Shred meat with two forks; return to the slow cooker and heat through. Spoon 1/2 cup onto each hamburger bun; top with a slice of pineapple. **Yield:** 8 servings.

Tomato Hamburger Soup

(Pictured below)

Cook Time: 4 Hours

Julie Kruger, St. Cloud, Minnesota

As a full-time teacher who doesn't have a lot of time to cook, I like supper dishes that leave leftovers for the next day. This recipe makes a big enough batch to feed my family for 2 nights.

- 1 can (46 ounces) V8 juice
- 2 packages (16 ounces *each*) frozen mixed vegetables
- 1 pound ground beef, cooked and drained
- 1 can (10-3/4 ounces) condensed cream of mushroom soup, undiluted
- 2 teaspoons dried minced onion

Salt and pepper to taste

In a 5-qt. slow cooker, combine the first five ingredients; mix well. Cover and cook on high for 4 hours or until heated through. Season with salt and pepper. **Yield:** 12 servings (3 quarts).

Tomato Hamburger Soup

Veggie Soup Is Versatile

For a change of pace, vary the flavor of easy-to-fix Tomato Hamburger Soup (recipe above right) each time you prepare it. Simply use different blends of frozen mixed vegetables.

Pork and Veggie Soup

Cook Time: 7 to 8 Hours

Jennifer Honeycutt, Nashville, Tennessee

Looking for a change from typical vegetable beef soup? Try this hearty combination. The tasty broth has tender chunks of pork and a bounty of veggies.

    2 pounds boneless pork, cubed
    2 tablespoons vegetable oil
    2 cups water
    4 medium carrots, cut into 1-inch pieces
    1 can (14-1/2 ounces) diced tomatoes,
      undrained
1-1/2 cups frozen corn
1-1/2 cups frozen cut green beans
    1 large onion, chopped
    1 jar (8 ounces) salsa
    1 can (4 ounces) chopped green chilies
    1 tablespoon minced fresh parsley
    2 garlic cloves, minced
    2 teaspoons beef bouillon granules
    2 teaspoons ground cumin
  1/2 teaspoon salt
  1/2 teaspoon pepper

In a large skillet, brown pork in oil over medium heat; drain. Transfer to a slow cooker. Stir in the remaining ingredients. Cover and cook on low for 7-8 hours or until meat juices run clear and vegetables are tender. **Yield:** 9 servings.

Hearty Black Bean Soup

Cook Time: 9 to 10 Hours

Amy Chop, Oak Grove, Louisiana

If you have smoked sausage, browned ground beef or a roast, toss it in this soup for the last 30 minutes of cooking. I serve this delicious soup over rice.

    3 medium carrots, halved and thinly sliced
    2 celery ribs, thinly sliced
    1 medium onion, chopped
    4 garlic cloves, minced
    1 can (30 ounces) black beans, rinsed and
      drained
    2 cans (14-1/2 ounces *each*) chicken broth
    1 can (15 ounces) crushed tomatoes
1-1/2 teaspoons dried basil
  1/2 teaspoon dried oregano
  1/2 teaspoon ground cumin
  1/2 teaspoon chili powder
  1/2 teaspoon hot pepper sauce
Hot cooked rice

In a slow cooker, combine the first 12 ingredients. Cover and cook on low for 9-10 hours or until vegetables are tender. Serve over rice. **Yield:** 8 servings.

Shredded Barbecued Beef

Shredded Barbecued Beef

(Pictured above)

Cook Time: 6 to 8 Hours

Jan Walls, Camden, Delaware

I work for the Delaware Department of Transportation and have prepared this simple main course during storm emergencies. Everyone's satisfied when I serve up this flavorful shredded beef on sandwich rolls.

    1 teaspoon celery salt
    1 teaspoon garlic powder
    1 teaspoon onion powder
    1 fresh beef brisket (3 to 5 pounds), halved
    3 tablespoons Liquid Smoke, optional
    1 tablespoon hot pepper sauce
    1 bottle (18 ounces) barbecue sauce
   12 sandwich rolls, split

Combine the celery salt, garlic powder and onion powder; rub over brisket. Place in a 5-qt. slow cooker. Combine Liquid Smoke if desired and hot pepper sauce; pour over brisket. Cover and cook on low for 6-8 hours or until the meat is tender.

Remove roast and cool slightly. Strain cooking juices, reserving 1/2 cup. Shred meat with two forks; place in a large saucepan. Add the barbecue sauce and reserved cooking juices; heat through. Serve about 1/3 cup meat mixture on each roll. **Yield:** 12 servings.

Editor's Note: This is a fresh beef brisket, not corned beef.

Stews &
Chili

Southwest Turkey Stew (p. 40)

Chapter 3

Chicken Chili

(Pictured below)

Cook Time: 5 Hours

Here's a tasty new take on an old-time classic from the Taste of Home Test Kitchen. Chili gets a makeover with chicken, white beans and a hint of coriander.

1-1/2 **pounds boneless skinless chicken breasts, cut into 1/2-inch cubes**
1 **cup chopped onion**
3 **tablespoons vegetable oil**
1 **can (15 ounces) cannellini** *or* **white kidney beans, rinsed and drained**
1 **can (14-1/2 ounces) diced tomatoes, undrained**
1 **can (14-1/2 ounces) diced tomatoes with mild green chilies, undrained**
1 **cup frozen corn**
1 **teaspoon salt**
1 **teaspoon ground cumin**
1 **teaspoon minced garlic**
1/2 **teaspoon celery salt**
1/2 **teaspoon ground coriander**
1/2 **teaspoon pepper**
Sour cream and shredded cheddar cheese, optional

In a large skillet, saute chicken and onion in oil for 5 minutes or until chicken is browned. Transfer to a 5-qt. slow cooker. Stir in the beans, tomatoes, corn and seasonings. Cover and cook on low for 5 hours or until chicken is no longer pink. Garnish with sour cream and cheese if desired. **Yield:** 6 servings.

Meatball Stew

Meatball Stew

(Pictured above)

Cook Time: 9 to 10 Hours

Iris Schultz, Miamisburg, Ohio

I came up with this hearty meal-in-one as another way to use frozen meatballs. It's quick to put together in the morning.

3 **medium potatoes, peeled and cut into 1/2-inch cubes**
1 **package (16 ounces) fresh baby carrots, quartered**
1 **large onion, chopped**
3 **celery ribs, sliced**
1 **package (12 ounces) frozen fully cooked meatballs**
1 **can (10-3/4 ounces) condensed tomato soup, undiluted**
1 **can (10-1/2 ounces) beef gravy**
1 **cup water**
1 **envelope onion soup mix**
2 **teaspoons beef bouillon granules**

Place the potatoes, carrots, onion, celery and meatballs in a 5-qt. slow cooker. In a bowl, combine the remaining ingredients. Pour over meatball mixture. Cover and cook on low for 9-10 hours or until the vegetables are crisp-tender. **Yield:** 6 servings.

Chicken Chili

Spicy Pork Chili

(Pictured below)

Cook Time: 6 Hours

With plenty of cayenne pepper and chili powder, this recipe from our Test Kitchen lives up to its name.

- 2 **pounds boneless pork, cut into 1/2-inch cubes**
- 1 **tablespoon vegetable oil**
- 1 **can (28 ounces) crushed tomatoes**
- 2 **cups frozen corn**
- 1 **can (15 ounces) black beans, rinsed and drained**
- 1 **cup chopped onion**
- 1 **cup beef broth**
- 1 **can (4 ounces) chopped green chilies**
- 1 **tablespoon chili powder**
- 1 **teaspoon minced garlic**
- 1/2 **teaspoon salt**
- 1/2 **teaspoon cayenne pepper**
- 1/2 **teaspoon pepper**
- 1/4 **cup minced fresh cilantro**

Shredded cheddar cheese, optional

In a large skillet, cook pork in oil over medium-high heat for 5-6 minutes or until browned. Transfer pork and drippings to a 5-qt. slow cooker.

Stir in the tomatoes, corn, beans, onion, broth, chilies, chili powder, garlic, salt, cayenne and pepper. Cover and cook on low for 6 hours or until pork is tender. Stir in cilantro. Serve with cheese if desired. **Yield:** 6 servings.

Southwestern Stew

Cook Time: 6 Hours

Virginia Price, Cheyenne, Wyoming

Slow cooking allows the flavors in this rave-winning recipe to blend beautifully. Loaded with pork, tomatoes, onion and yellow hominy, the stew has become a tradition in our household. In fact, steaming bowls of this hearty dish are a must for our Super Bowl Sunday meal. Watching the football game just wouldn't be the same without them!

- 1-1/2 **pounds boneless pork, trimmed and cut into 1/2-inch cubes**
- 2 **tablespoons vegetable oil**
- 1 **medium onion, chopped**
- 1 **can (15-1/2 ounces) yellow hominy, drained**
- 1 **can (14-1/2 ounces) diced tomatoes, undrained**
- 1 **can (4 ounces) chopped green chilies**
- 1/2 **cup water**
- 1/2 **teaspoon chili powder**
- 1/4 **teaspoon garlic powder**
- 1/4 **teaspoon ground cumin**
- 1/4 **teaspoon salt**
- 1/4 **teaspoon pepper**

In a large skillet over medium-high heat, brown pork in oil. Add onion and cook for 2 minutes or until tender.

Transfer to a slow cooker; add the remaining ingredients. Cover and cook on high for 2 hours. Reduce heat to low and cook 4 hours longer. **Yield:** 4-6 servings.

Spicy Pork Chili

Creamy Bratwurst Stew

and water until smooth; stir into stew. Cover and cook on high for 30 minutes or until the gravy is thickened. **Yield:** 8 servings.

Creamy Bratwurst Stew

(Pictured above)

Cook Time: 7-1/2 Hours

Susan Holmes, Germantown, Wisconsin

A rich cream sauce coats this hearty combination of potatoes, carrots, bratwurst chunks and more. It is so comforting on cold evenings. If you like, round out the meal with a tossed green salad and your favorite fresh-from-the-oven bread.

> 4 medium potatoes, cubed
> 2 medium carrots, coarsely chopped
> 2 celery ribs, chopped
> 1 cup chopped onion
> 3/4 cup chopped green pepper
> 2 pounds fresh bratwurst links, cut into 1-inch slices
> 1/2 cup chicken broth
> 1 teaspoon salt
> 1 teaspoon dried basil
> 1/2 teaspoon pepper
> 2 cups half-and-half cream
> 3 tablespoons cornstarch
> 3 teaspoons cold water

In a 5-qt. slow cooker, combine the potatoes, carrots, celery, onion and green pepper. Top with bratwurst slices. Combine the broth, salt, basil and pepper; pour over top. Cover and cook on low for 7 hours or until vegetables are tender and sausage is no longer pink.

Stir in half-and-half cream. Combine cornstarch

Smoky Bean Stew

Cook Time: 4 to 5 Hours

Glenda Holmes, Riley, Kansas

I get this satisfying stew started in the slow cooker, then spend the afternoon curled up with a good book! When dinnertime rolls around, I have a fantastic meal-in-one that's cooked and ready to serve.

> 1 package (16 ounces) miniature smoked sausage links
> 1 can (16 ounces) baked beans
> 2 cups frozen cut green beans
> 2 cups frozen lima beans
> 1/2 cup packed brown sugar
> 1/2 cup thinly sliced carrot
> 1/2 cup chopped onion
> 1/2 cup ketchup
> 1 tablespoon cider vinegar
> 1 teaspoon prepared mustard

In a 3-qt. slow cooker, combine all ingredients. Cover and cook on high for 4-5 hours or until vegetables are tender. **Yield:** 6-8 servings.

French Beef Stew

Cook Time: 9 to 10 Hours

Iola Egle, Bella Vista, Arkansas

I let the slow cooker do the work for this down-home stew. The vegetables and seasonings combine beautifully, and the result is a memorable main dish that never fails to please. This is one of the most-used recipes in my file.

> 3 medium potatoes, peeled and cut into 1/2-inch cubes
> 2 pounds beef stew meat
> 4 medium carrots, sliced
> 2 medium onions, sliced
> 3 celery ribs, sliced
> 2 cups tomato juice
> 1 cup water
> 1/3 cup quick-cooking tapioca
> 1 tablespoon sugar
> 1 tablespoon salt
> 1 teaspoon dried basil
> 1/2 teaspoon pepper

Place the potatoes in a greased 5-qt. slow cooker. Top with the beef, carrots, onions and celery. In a bowl, combine the remaining ingredients. Pour over the vegetables. Cover and cook on low for 9-10 hours or until vegetables and beef are tender. **Yield:** 8-10 servings.

Sausage Pasta Stew

(Pictured below)

Cook Time: 7-1/4 to 9-1/4 Hours

Sara Bowen, Upland, California

Packed with turkey sausage, pasta and veggies, this is a healthy dish my family gobbles up gladly.

- 1 pound turkey Italian sausage links, casings removed
- 4 cups water
- 1 jar (26 ounces) meatless spaghetti sauce
- 1 can (16 ounces) kidney beans, rinsed and drained
- 1 medium yellow summer squash, halved lengthwise and cut into 1-inch pieces
- 2 medium carrots, cut into 1/4-inch slices
- 1 medium sweet red *or* green pepper, diced
- 1/3 cup chopped onion
- 1-1/2 cups uncooked spiral pasta
- 1 cup frozen peas
- 1 teaspoon sugar
- 1/2 teaspoon salt
- 1/4 teaspoon pepper

In a nonstick skillet, cook sausage over medium heat until no longer pink; drain and place in a 5-qt. slow cooker. Add water, spaghetti sauce, beans, summer squash, carrots, red pepper and onion; mix well. Cover and cook on low for 7-9 hours or until vegetables are tender.

Stir in the pasta, peas, sugar, salt and pepper; mix well. Cover and cook on high for 15-20 minutes or until pasta is tender. **Yield:** 8 servings.

Sausage Pasta Stew

Texas Stew

Texas Stew

(Pictured above)

Cook Time: 4 Hours

Kim Balstad, Lewisville, Texas

As a mother of young children, I rely on family-friendly recipes more and more. Everyone enjoys this stew.

- 1 can (15-1/2 ounces) hominy, drained
- 1 can (15-1/4 ounces) whole kernel corn, drained
- 1 can (15 ounces) sliced carrots, drained
- 1 can (15 ounces) sliced potatoes, drained
- 1 can (15 ounces) ranch-style *or* chili beans, undrained
- 1 can (14-1/2 ounces) diced tomatoes, undrained
- 1 cup water
- 1 beef bouillon cube
- 1/2 teaspoon garlic powder
- Chili powder to taste
- Dash Worcestershire sauce
- Dash hot pepper sauce
- 1-1/2 pounds ground beef
- 1 medium onion, chopped

In a slow cooker, combine the first 12 ingredients. In a skillet, cook beef and onion over medium heat until meat is no longer pink; drain. Transfer to the slow cooker; mix well. Cover and cook on high for 4 hours or until heated through. **Yield:** 10-12 servings.

Santa Fe Chili

(Pictured below)

Cook Time: 4 Hours

Laura Manning, Lilburn, Georgia

This colorful chili is perfect for holiday get-togethers and casual suppers alike.

- 2 pounds ground beef
- 1 medium onion, chopped
- 2 cans (16 ounces *each*) kidney beans, rinsed and drained
- 2 cans (15 ounces *each*) black beans, rinsed and drained
- 2 cans (15 ounces *each*) pinto beans, rinsed and drained
- 2 cans (11 ounces *each*) shoepeg corn, drained
- 1 can (14-1/2 ounces) diced tomatoes, undrained
- 1 can (10 ounces) diced tomatoes with mild green chilies, undrained
- 1 can (11-1/2 ounces) V8 juice
- 2 envelopes ranch salad dressing mix
- 2 envelopes taco seasoning

Sour cream, shredded cheddar cheese and tortilla chips, optional

In a large skillet, cook beef and onion over medium heat until meat is no longer pink; drain. Transfer to a 5-qt. slow cooker. Stir in the beans, corn, tomatoes, V8 juice, salad dressing mix and taco seasoning. Cover and cook on high for 4 hours or until heated through. Serve with sour cream, cheese and tortilla chips if desired. **Yield:** 4 quarts (16 servings).

Chicken Stew

Cook Time: 4-1/2 Hours

Linda Emery, Tuckerman, Arkansas

Simmer this yummy stew to perfection while you're raking leaves or picking pumpkins.

- 2 pounds boneless skinless chicken breasts, cut into 1-inch cubes
- 2 cans (14-1/2 ounces *each*) chicken broth
- 3 cups cubed peeled potatoes
- 1 cup chopped onion
- 1 cup sliced celery
- 1 cup thinly sliced carrots
- 1 teaspoon paprika
- 1/2 teaspoon pepper
- 1/2 teaspoon rubbed sage
- 1/2 teaspoon dried thyme
- 1 can (6 ounces) tomato paste
- 1/4 cup cold water
- 3 tablespoons cornstarch

In a slow cooker, combine the first 11 ingredients; cover and cook on high for 4 hours. Mix water and cornstarch until smooth; stir into stew. Cook, covered, 30 minutes more or until the vegetables are tender. **Yield:** 10 servings.

Country Cassoulet

Cook Time: 5 to 6 Hours

Suzanne McKinley, Lyons, Georgia

This bean entree is great with fresh rolls and a green salad. It's a hearty meal that's perfect after a busy day.

- 1 pound (2 cups) dry great northern beans
- 2 fresh garlic sausage links
- 3 bacon strips, diced
- 1-1/2 pounds boneless pork, cut into 1-inch cubes
- 1 pound boneless lamb, cut into 1-inch cubes
- 1-1/2 cups chopped onion
- 3 garlic cloves, minced
- 2 teaspoons salt
- 1 teaspoon dried thyme
- 4 whole cloves
- 2 bay leaves
- 2-1/2 cups chicken broth
- 1 can (8 ounces) tomato sauce

Place beans and enough water to cover in a Dutch oven or soup kettle. Bring to a boil; boil for 2 minutes. Remove from the heat and let stand for 1 hour. Drain beans and discard liquid. In a large skillet over

Sante Fe Chili

Barbecued Turkey Chili

Zippy Bean Stew

(Pictured below)

Cook Time: 4 to 5 Hours

Debbie Matthews, Bluefield, West Virginia

Full of flavor, this bean stew is a staple for my coworkers and me once the weather turns cool.

- 1 can (14-1/2 ounces) vegetable *or* chicken broth
- 1 can (16 ounces) kidney beans, rinsed and drained
- 1 can (15 ounces) pinto beans, rinsed and drained
- 1 can (14-1/2 ounces) diced tomatoes and green chilies
- 1 can (4 ounces) chopped green chilies, undrained
- 1 package (10 ounces) frozen corn, thawed
- 3 cups water
- 1 large onion, chopped
- 2 medium carrots, sliced
- 2 garlic cloves, minced
- 2 teaspoons chili powder

Combine all ingredients in a slow cooker. Cover and cook on high for 4-5 hours or until heated through and flavors are blended. **Yield:** 6 servings.

medium-high heat, brown sausage; remove with a slotted spoon to a slow cooker. Add bacon to skillet; cook until crisp. Remove with a slotted spoon to slow cooker. In bacon drippings, cook pork and lamb until browned on all sides. Remove pork and lamb with a slotted spoon to slow cooker. Stir in beans and remaining ingredients.

Cover and cook on high for 2 hours. Reduce heat to low and cook 3-4 hours longer. Remove cloves and bay leaves. Remove sausage and slice into 1/4-in. pieces; return to slow cooker and stir gently. **Yield:** 8-10 servings.

Barbecued Turkey Chili

(Pictured above)

Cook Time: 4 Hours

Melissa Webb, Ellsworth Air Force Base, South Dakota

The first time I made this, it won the grand prize at a chili cook-off. It's often requested by friends and family.

- 1 can (16 ounces) kidney beans, rinsed and drained
- 1 can (15-1/2 ounces) hot chili beans
- 1 can (15 ounces) turkey chili with beans
- 1 can (14-1/2 ounces) diced tomatoes, undrained
- 1/3 cup barbecue sauce

In a 3-qt. slow cooker, combine all of the ingredients. Cover and cook on high for 4 hours or until heated through and flavors are blended. **Yield:** 4-6 servings.

Zippy Bean Stew

Southwest Turkey Stew

Sweet Potato Lentil Stew

Cook Time: 5 to 6 Hours

Heather Gray, Little Rock, Arkansas

Years ago, I fell in love with the spicy flavor and wonderful aroma of this satisfying slow-cooker recipe. You can serve the stew alone or as a topping for meat and poultry.

>   4 cups vegetable broth
>   3 cups sweet potatoes, peeled and cubed
>   (about 1-1/4 pounds)
> 1-1/2 cups lentils, rinsed
>   3 medium carrots, cut into 1-inch pieces
>   1 medium onion, chopped
>   4 garlic cloves, minced
>   1/2 teaspoon ground cumin
>   1/4 teaspoon ground ginger
>   1/4 teaspoon cayenne pepper
>   1/4 cup minced fresh cilantro
>   1/4 teaspoon salt

In a slow cooker, combine the first nine ingredients. Cover and cook on low for 5-6 hours or until vegetables are tender. Stir in the cilantro and salt. **Yield:** 6 servings.

Southwest Turkey Stew

(Pictured above and on page 32)

Cook Time: 5 to 6 Hours

Stephanie Wilson, Helix, Oregon

This dish enables me to stay on my diet but still eat what the rest of the family eats. Everyone loves it.

> 1-1/2 pounds turkey tenderloins, cubed
>   2 teaspoons canola oil
>   1 can (15 ounces) turkey chili with beans,
>   undrained
>   1 can (14-1/2 ounces) diced tomatoes,
>   undrained
>   1 medium sweet red pepper, cut into 3/4-inch
>   pieces
>   1 medium green pepper, cut into 3/4-inch
>   pieces
>   3/4 cup chopped onion
>   3/4 cup salsa
>   3 garlic cloves, minced
> 1-1/2 teaspoons chili powder
>   1/2 teaspoon salt
>   1/2 teaspoon ground cumin
>   1 tablespoon minced fresh cilantro, optional

In a nonstick skillet, brown turkey in oil; transfer to a 3-qt. slow cooker. Stir in the chili, tomatoes, peppers, onion, salsa, garlic, chili powder, salt and cumin. Cover and cook on low for 5-6 hours or until turkey juices run clear. Garnish with cilantro if desired. **Yield:** 6 servings.

Two-Bean White Chili

Cook Time: 6 to 7 Hours

Shari Meissner, Chester, Montana

Plenty of cilantro, green chilies and ground cumin make this chicken chili a real winner.

>   3 medium onions, chopped
>   2 garlic cloves, minced
>   1 tablespoon olive oil
>   4 cups cubed cooked chicken *or* turkey
>   2 cans (15 ounces each) white kidney *or*
>   cannellini beans, rinsed and drained
>   1 can (15 ounces) garbanzo beans *or*
>   chickpeas, rinsed and drained
>   2 cups chicken broth
>   1 can (4 ounces) chopped green chilies
>   2 teaspoons ground cumin
>   1/2 teaspoon dried oregano
>   1/4 teaspoon salt
>   1/4 teaspoon cayenne pepper
>   1/4 cup minced fresh cilantro
> Corn chips, shredded Monterey Jack cheese and
>   sour cream

In a skillet, saute the onions and garlic in oil until tender. Transfer to a slow cooker. Add the chicken, beans, broth, green chilies, cumin, oregano, salt and cayenne; stir well. Cover and cook on low for 6-7 hours or until bubbly.

Stir in cilantro. Serve over corn chips; top with cheese and sour cream. **Yield:** 8 servings (2 quarts).

Mushroom Salsa Chili

(Pictured below)

Cook Time: 8 to 9 Hours

Richard Rundels, Waverly, Ohio

Green, red and yellow peppers give this hearty chili a splash of color. I often fix it for my grandsons. Because they don't like spicy chili, I use mild salsa.

- 1 pound ground beef
- 1 pound bulk pork sausage
- 2 cans (16 ounces *each*) kidney beans, rinsed and drained
- 1 jar (24 ounces) chunky salsa
- 1 can (14-1/2 ounces) diced tomatoes, undrained
- 1 large onion, chopped
- 1 can (8 ounces) tomato sauce
- 1 can (4 ounces) mushroom stems and pieces, drained
- 1/2 cup *each* chopped green pepper, sweet red and yellow pepper
- 1/2 teaspoon dried oregano
- 1/4 teaspoon garlic powder
- 1/8 teaspoon dried thyme
- 1/8 teaspoon dried marjoram

In a large skillet, cook beef and sausage over medium heat until meat is no longer pink; drain. Transfer meat to a 5-qt. slow cooker. Stir in the remaining ingredients. Cover and cook on low for 8-9 hours or until vegetables are tender. **Yield:** 8 servings.

Zippy Steak Chili

Mushroom Salsa Chili

Zippy Steak Chili

(Pictured above)

Cook Time: 6 to 8 Hours

Denise Habib, Poolesville, Maryland

Looking for a thick, chunky chili with a little extra-special kick for Super Bowl Sunday? I've made this recipe on numerous occasions and always get rave reviews.

- 1 pound boneless beef sirloin steak, cut into 1/2-inch cubes
- 1/2 cup chopped onion
- 2 tablespoons canola oil
- 2 tablespoons chili powder
- 1 teaspoon garlic powder
- 1 teaspoon ground cumin
- 1 teaspoon dried oregano
- 1 teaspoon pepper
- 2 cans (10 ounces *each*) diced tomatoes and green chilies, undrained
- 1 can (15-1/2 ounces) chili starter

Shredded cheddar cheese, chopped onion and sour cream, optional

In a large skillet, cook steak and onion in oil over medium heat until meat is no longer pink. Sprinkle with seasonings.

In a 5-qt. slow cooker, combine the tomatoes and chili starter. Stir in beef mixture. Cover and cook on low for 6-8 hours or until meat is tender. Serve with cheese, onion and sour cream if desired. **Yield:** 5 servings.

Editor's Note: This recipe was tested with Bush's Traditional Chili Starter.

Vegetable Beef Stew

Vegetable Beef Stew

(Pictured above)

Cook Time: 5-1/2 to 6-1/2 Hours

Ruth Rodriguez, Fort Myers Beach, Florida

Here is a tasty variation of beef stew that I came across. With sweet flavor from apricots and squash, we think it has South American or Cuban flair.

- 3/4 **pound lean beef stew meat, cut into 1/2-inch cubes**
- 2 **teaspoons canola oil**
- 1 **can (14-1/2 ounces) beef broth**
- 1 **can (14-1/2 ounces) stewed tomatoes, cut up**
- 1-1/2 **cups cubed peeled butternut squash**
- 1 **cup frozen corn, thawed**
- 6 **dried apricot *or* peach halves, quartered**
- 1/2 **cup chopped carrot**
- 1 **teaspoon dried oregano**
- 1/4 **teaspoon salt**
- 1/4 **teaspoon pepper**
- 2 **tablespoons cornstarch**
- 1/4 **cup water**
- 2 **tablespoons minced fresh parsley**

In a nonstick skillet, brown beef in oil over medium heat. Transfer to a slow cooker. Add the broth, tomatoes, squash, corn, apricots, carrot, oregano, salt and pepper. Cover and cook on high for 5-6 hours or until vegetables and meat are tender.

Combine cornstarch and water until smooth; stir into stew. Cover and cook on high for 30 minutes or until gravy is thickened. Stir in parsley. **Yield:** 4 servings.

Ham and Bean Stew

Cook Time: 7 Hours

Teresa D'Amato, East Granby, Connecticut

This thick stew is easy to make and often requested at my house. I top bowls of it with grated cheese.

- 2 **cans (16 ounces *each*) baked beans**
- 2 **medium potatoes, peeled and cubed**
- 2 **cups cubed fully cooked ham**
- 1 **celery rib, chopped**
- 1/2 **cup water**

In a slow cooker, combine all ingredients; mix well. Cover and cook on low for 7 hours or until the potatoes are tender. **Yield:** 6 servings.

Spicy Seafood Stew

(Pictured below)

Cook Time: 4-3/4 to 5-1/4 Hours

Bonnie Marlow, Ottoville, Ohio

The hardest part of making this zesty stew is peeling and dicing the potatoes, and that can be done ahead of time.

- 2 **pounds potatoes, peeled and diced**
- 1 **pound carrots, sliced**
- 1 **jar (26 ounces) spaghetti sauce**
- 2 **jars (6 ounces *each*) sliced mushrooms, drained**
- 1-1/2 **teaspoons ground turmeric**
- 1-1/2 **teaspoons minced garlic**
- 1 **teaspoon cayenne pepper**
- 3/4 **teaspoon salt**
- 1-1/2 **cups water**
- 1 **pound sea scallops**
- 1 **pound uncooked medium shrimp, peeled and deveined**

Spicy Seafood Stew

In a 5-qt. slow cooker, combine the first eight ingredients. Cover and cook on low for 4-1/2 to 5 hours or until potatoes are tender.

Stir in the water, scallops and shrimp. Cover and cook for 15-20 minutes or until scallops are opaque and shrimp turn pink. **Yield:** 9 servings.

Cabbage Patch Stew

Cook Time: 6 to 8 Hours

Karen Ann Bland, Gove, Kansas

Our family can't get enough of this stick-to-your-ribs dish. I like to serve steaming helpings in old-fashioned soup plates with thick, crusty slices of homemade bread.

- 1 **pound ground beef**
- 1 **cup chopped onion**
- 2 **celery ribs, chopped**
- 11 **cups chopped cabbage**
- 2 **cans (14-1/2 ounces** *each***) stewed tomatoes**
- 1 **can (15 ounces) pinto beans, rinsed and drained**
- 1 **can (10 ounces) diced tomatoes with green chilies**
- 1/2 **cup ketchup**
- 1 **to 1-1/2 teaspoons chili powder**
- 1/2 **teaspoon dried oregano**
- 1/2 **teaspoon pepper**
- 1/4 **teaspoon salt**

Shredded cheddar cheese and sour cream, optional

In a large skillet, cook the beef, onion and celery over medium heat until meat is no longer pink and vegetables are tender; drain. Transfer to a 5-qt. slow cooker. Stir in cabbage, stewed tomatoes, beans, diced tomatoes, ketchup, chili powder, oregano, pepper and salt. Cover and cook on low for 6-8 hours or until cabbage is tender. Serve with cheese and sour cream if desired. **Yield:** 8 servings.

Colony Mountain Chili

(Pictured above right)

Cook Time: 6 to 8 Hours

Marjorie O'Dell, Bow, Washington

My husband created this chili for a local cooking contest, and it won the People's Choice award. It's loaded with beef, Italian sausage, tomatoes and beans.

- 1 **pound boneless beef sirloin steak, cut into 3/4-inch cubes**
- 4 **Italian sausage links, casings removed and cut into 3/4-inch slices**
- 2 **tablespoons olive oil,** *divided*
- 1 **medium onion, chopped**
- 3 **garlic cloves, minced**
- 2 **green onions, thinly sliced**

Colony Mountain Chili

- 2 **teaspoons beef bouillon granules**
- 1 **cup boiling water**
- 1 **can (6 ounces) tomato paste**
- 3 **tablespoons chili powder**
- 2 **tablespoons brown sugar**
- 2 **tablespoons Worcestershire sauce**
- 2 **teaspoons ground cumin**
- 1 **to 2 teaspoons crushed red pepper flakes**
- 1 **teaspoon salt**
- 1/2 **teaspoon pepper**
- 3 **cans (14-1/2 ounces** *each***) stewed tomatoes, cut up**
- 2 **cans (15 ounces** *each***) pinto beans, rinsed and drained**

Shredded cheddar cheese, optional

In a large skillet, brown the beef and sausage in 1 tablespoon oil; drain. Transfer meat to a 5-qt. slow cooker. In the same skillet, saute the onion, garlic and green onions in remaining oil until tender. Transfer to slow cooker.

In a small bowl, dissolve bouillon in water. Stir in tomato paste, chili powder, brown sugar, Worcestershire sauce and seasonings until blended; add to slow cooker. Stir in tomatoes and beans. Cover and cook on high for 6-8 hours or until meat is tender. Serve with cheese if desired. **Yield:** 10 servings.

Serve a Speedy Side

To round out a meal featuring slow-cooked chili or stew, you can rely on a variety of refrigerated breads. Keep tubes of crescent rolls, corn bread twists, crusty French loaf and dinner rolls on hand. When your main dish is nearing the end of its cooking time, pop your bread in the oven for the perfect accompaniment.

Beef &
Ground Beef

Fabulous Fajitas (p. 49)

Chapter 4

Beef 'n' Bean Torta

(Pictured below)

Cook Time: 4 to 5 Hours

Joan Hallford, North Richland Hills, Texas

This zesty dish is a favorite of mine because it has a wonderful southwestern taste and is a breeze to prepare.

> 1 **pound ground beef**
> 1 **small onion, chopped**
> 1 **can (15 ounces) pinto *or* black beans, rinsed and drained**
> 1 **can (10 ounces) diced tomatoes and green chilies, undrained**
> 1 **can (2-1/4 ounces) sliced ripe olives, drained**
> 1-1/2 **teaspoons chili powder**
> 1/2 **teaspoon salt**
> 1/8 **teaspoon pepper**
> 3 **drops hot pepper sauce**
> 4 **flour tortillas (8 inches)**
> 1 **cup (4 ounces) shredded cheddar cheese**

Minced fresh cilantro, optional
Salsa, sour cream, shredded lettuce and chopped tomatoes, optional

Cut four 20-in. x 3-in. strips of heavy-duty foil; crisscross so they resemble spokes of a wheel. Place strips on the bottom and up the sides of a 5-qt. slow cooker. Coat strips with nonstick cooking spray.

In a large skillet, cook beef and onion over medium heat until meat is no longer pink; drain. Stir in the beans, tomatoes, olives, chili powder, salt, pepper and hot pepper sauce. Spoon about 1-2/3 cups into prepared slow cooker; top with one tortilla and 1/4 cup cheese. Repeat layers three times.

Cover and cook on low for 4-5 hours or until heated through. Using foil strips as handles, remove the tortilla stack to a platter. Sprinkle with cilantro. Serve with salsa, sour cream, lettuce and tomatoes if desired. **Yield:** 4 servings.

Slow-Cooked Cabbage Rolls

Cook Time: 6 to 7 Hours

Rosemary Jarvis, Sparta, Tennessee

I've worked full-time for more than 30 years, and this super slow-cooker recipe has been a lifesaver.

> 1 **large head cabbage**
> 1 **egg, beaten**
> 1 **can (8 ounces) tomato sauce**
> 3/4 **cup quick-cooking rice**
> 1/2 **cup chopped green pepper**
> 1/2 **cup crushed saltines (about 15 crackers)**
> 1 **envelope onion soup mix**
> 1-1/2 **pounds lean ground beef**
> 1 **can (46 ounces) V8 juice**

Salt to taste
Grated Parmesan cheese, optional

Remove core from cabbage. Steam 12 large outer leaves until limp; drain well. In a bowl, combine the egg, tomato sauce, rice, green pepper, cracker crumbs and soup mix. Crumble beef over mixture and mix well. Place about 1/3 cup meat mixture on each cabbage leaf. Fold in sides, starting at an unfolded edge, and roll up completely to enclose the filling. Secure with toothpicks if desired.

Place cabbage rolls in a slow cooker. Pour V8 juice over rolls. Cover and cook on low for 6-7 hours or until filling reaches 160°. Just before serving, sprinkle with salt and cheese if desired. **Yield:** 6 servings.

Beef 'n' Bean Torta

Beef & Ground Beef

Special Flank Steak

(Pictured at right)

Cook Time: 8 to 10 Hours

Kathy Clark, Byron, Minnesota

This recipe came with my first slow cooker. I'm currently on my fourth slow cooker, but I still turn to this impressive main course.

- **1 beef flank steak (2 pounds)**
- **1 medium onion, chopped**
- **1 garlic clove, minced**
- **1 tablespoon butter**
- **1-1/2 cups soft bread crumbs (about 3 slices)**
- **1/2 cup chopped fresh mushrooms**
- **1/4 cup minced fresh parsley**
- **1/4 cup egg substitute**
- **3/4 teaspoon poultry seasoning**
- **1/2 teaspoon salt**
- **1/8 teaspoon pepper**
- **1/2 cup beef broth**
- **2 teaspoons cornstarch**
- **4 teaspoons water**

Special Flank Steak

Flatten steak to 1/2-in. thickness; set aside. In a nonstick skillet, saute onion and garlic in butter until tender. Add the bread crumbs, mushrooms, parsley, egg substitute, poultry seasoning, salt and pepper; mix well. Spread over steak to within 1 in. of edge. Roll up jelly-roll style, starting with a long side; tie with kitchen string. Place in a 5-qt. slow cooker; add broth. Cover and cook on low for 8-10 hours.

Remove meat to a serving platter and keep warm. Skim fat from cooking juices; pour into a small saucepan. Combine cornstarch and water until smooth; stir into juices. Bring to a boil; cook and stir for 1-2 minutes or until thickened. Remove string before slicing steak; serve with gravy. **Yield: 8 servings.**

Party-Pleasing Beef Dish

Cook Time: 4-1/4 Hours

Glee Witzke, Crete, Nebraska

I often prepare this spaghetti sauce-like mixture when guests are coming. It's easy to fix and easy to serve with tortilla chips and toppings.

- **1 pound ground beef**
- **1 medium onion, chopped**
- **3/4 cup water**
- **1 can (8 ounces) tomato sauce**
- **1 can (6 ounces) tomato paste**
- **2 teaspoons sugar**
- **1 garlic clove, minced**
- **1 teaspoon chili powder**
- **1 teaspoon ground cumin**
- **1 teaspoon dried oregano**
- **1 cup cooked rice**

Tortilla chips
Toppings—shredded cheddar cheese, chopped green onions, sliced ripe olives, sour cream, chopped tomato and taco sauce

In a large skillet, cook beef and onion over medium heat until meat is no longer pink; drain. Transfer to a slow cooker. Add the next eight ingredients; mix well. Cover and cook on low for 4 hours or until heated through. Add rice; cover and cook 10 minutes longer. Serve over tortilla chips with toppings of your choice. **Yield: 6-8 servings.**

Onion Meat Loaf

Cook Time: 5 to 6 Hours

Rhonda Cowden, Quincy, Illinois

My husband and I really enjoy this delicious meat loaf. You need just five ingredients to assemble the simple entree.

- **2 eggs**
- **1/2 cup ketchup**
- **3/4 cup quick-cooking oats**
- **1 envelope onion soup mix**
- **2 pounds ground beef**

In a large bowl, combine the eggs, ketchup, oats and soup mix. Crumble beef over mixture; mix well. Shape into a round loaf.

Cut three 20-in. x 3-in. strips of heavy-duty aluminum foil. Crisscross the strips so they resemble the spokes of a wheel. Place meat loaf in the center of the strips; pull the strips up and bend the edges to form handles. Grasp the foil handles to transfer loaf to a 3-qt. slow cooker. (Leave the foil in while meat loaf cooks.)

Cover and cook on low for 5-6 hours or until a meat thermometer reaches 160°. Using foil strips, lift meat loaf out of slow cooker. **Yield: 8 servings.**

Slow Cooker Beef Au Jus

Slow Cooker Beef Au Jus

(Pictured above)

Cook Time: 6 to 7 Hours

Carol Hille, Grand Junction, Colorado

This simple roast has lots of onion flavor. Sometimes I also add cubed potatoes and baby carrots to the slow cooker.

- 1 boneless beef rump roast (3 pounds)
- 1 large onion, sliced
- 3/4 cup beef broth
- 1 envelope (1 ounce) au jus gravy mix
- 2 garlic cloves, halved
- 1/4 teaspoon pepper

Cut roast in half. In a large nonstick skillet coated with nonstick cooking spray, brown meat on all sides over medium-high heat. Place onion in a 5-qt. slow cooker. Top with meat. Combine the broth, gravy mix, garlic and pepper. Pour over meat. Cover and cook on low for 6-7 hours or until meat and onion are tender.

Remove meat to a cutting board. Let stand for 10 minutes. Thinly slice meat and return to slow cooker. Serve meat with pan juices and onions. **Yield: 10 servings.**

Beef 'n' Chili Beans

Cook Time: 6 to 8 Hours

Anita Hudson, Savoy, Texas

I took this dish to the last church meal I attended, and it was a big hit. People loved the southwestern flavor.

- 3 pounds beef stew meat, cut into 1-inch cubes
- 2 tablespoons brown sugar

1-1/2 teaspoons ground mustard
- 1 teaspoon salt
- 1 teaspoon paprika
- 1/2 teaspoon chili powder
- 1/4 teaspoon pepper
- 1 large onion, chopped
- 2 cans (10 ounces *each*) diced tomatoes and green chilies
- 1 can (15-1/2 ounces) ranch-style beans *or* chili beans, undrained
- 1 can (15-1/4 ounces) whole kernel corn, drained

Place the beef in a 3-qt. slow cooker. Combine the brown sugar, mustard, salt, paprika, chili powder and pepper; sprinkle over beef and toss to coat. Top with the onion, tomatoes, beans and corn. Cover and cook on low for 6-8 hours or until the meat is tender. **Yield: 6-8 servings.**

Slow-Cooked Spaghetti Sauce

(Pictured below)

Cook Time: 7 to 8 Hours

Shelley McKinney, New Castle, Indiana

I like to serve this to company. Not only is it delicious and a snap to prepare, but it's economical, too.

- 1 pound ground beef *or* bulk Italian sausage
- 1 medium onion, chopped
- 2 cans (14-1/2 ounces *each*) diced tomatoes, undrained
- 1 can (8 ounces) tomato sauce
- 1 can (6 ounces) tomato paste
- 1 bay leaf

Slow-Cooked Spaghetti Sauce

1 tablespoon brown sugar
4 garlic cloves, minced
1 to 2 teaspoons dried basil
1 to 2 teaspoons dried oregano
1 teaspoon salt
1/2 to 1 teaspoon dried thyme
Hot cooked spaghetti

In a skillet, cook beef and onion over medium heat until meat is no longer pink; drain. Transfer to a slow cooker. Add the next 10 ingredients. Cover and cook on low for 7-8 hours or until heated through. Discard bay leaf. Serve over spaghetti. **Yield:** 6-8 servings.

Barbecued Beef Brisket

(Pictured on back cover)

Cook Time: 4 to 5 Hours

Anita Keppinger, Philomath, Oregon

I enjoy fixing a sit-down meal for my husband and myself every evening, so this entree is often on the menu.

1 teaspoon salt
1 teaspoon chili powder
1/2 teaspoon garlic powder
1/4 teaspoon onion powder
1/4 teaspoon celery seed
1/4 teaspoon pepper
1 fresh beef brisket (2-1/2 pounds), trimmed
SAUCE:
1/2 cup ketchup
1/2 cup chili sauce
1/4 cup packed brown sugar
2 tablespoons cider vinegar
2 tablespoons Worcestershire sauce
1 to 1-1/2 teaspoons Liquid Smoke, optional
1/2 teaspoon ground mustard

Combine the first six ingredients; rub over brisket. Place in a slow cooker. In a bowl, combine the sauce ingredients. Pour half over the brisket; set the remaining sauce aside. Cover and cook on high for 4-5 hours or until meat is tender. Serve with the reserved sauce. **Yield:** 8 servings.

Editor's Note: This is a fresh beef brisket, not corned beef.

Fabulous Fajitas

Fabulous Fajitas

(Pictured above and on page 44)

Cook Time: 3-1/2 to 4 Hours

Janie Reitz, Rochester, Minnesota

I've enjoyed cooking ever since I was a girl growing up in the Southwest. When friends call to ask me for new recipes to try, I suggest these mouth-watering fajitas.

1-1/2 pounds boneless sirloin steak, cut into thin strips
2 tablespoons vegetable oil
2 tablespoons lemon juice
1 garlic clove, minced
1-1/2 teaspoons ground cumin
1 teaspoon seasoned salt
1/2 teaspoon chili powder
1/4 to 1/2 teaspoon crushed red pepper flakes
1 large green pepper, julienned
1 large onion, julienned
6 to 8 flour tortillas (7 inches)
Shredded cheddar cheese, salsa, sour cream, lettuce and tomatoes, optional

In a skillet over medium heat, brown the steak in oil. Place steak and drippings in a slow cooker. Add lemon juice, garlic, cumin, salt, chili powder and red pepper flakes; mix well. Cover and cook on high for 2-1/2 to 3 hours or until meat is tender. Add green pepper and onion; cover and cook for 1 hour or until vegetables are tender.

Warm tortillas according to package directions; spoon beef and vegetables down the center of tortillas. Top each with cheese, salsa, sour cream, lettuce and tomatoes if desired. Fold in sides of tortillas and serve immediately. **Yield:** 6-8 servings.

Hearty Beans with Beef

Cook Time: 3 to 4 Hours

Jan Biehl, Leesburg, Indiana

My husband raved about this sweet bean dish after tasting it at a party, so I knew I had to get the recipe.

- 1 pound ground beef
- 1 medium onion, chopped
- 1 can (16 ounces) baked beans, undrained
- 1 can (15-1/2 ounces) chili beans, undrained
- 1 can (15-1/2 ounces) butter beans, rinsed and drained
- 1/2 cup ketchup
- 1/3 cup packed brown sugar
- 1 tablespoon barbecue sauce
- 1/4 teaspoon Worcestershire sauce

In a large skillet, cook beef and onion over medium heat until meat is no longer pink; drain. Transfer to a slow cooker. Stir in the remaining ingredients. Cover and cook on high for 3-4 hours or until heated through. **Yield:** 8-10 servings.

Throw-Together Short Ribs

(Pictured below)

Cook Time: 4-1/4 to 5-1/4 Hours

Lamya Asiff, Delburne, Alberta

This recipe takes no time to prepare and results in the most terrific, fall-off-the-bone short ribs. The longer you cook them, the better they get! Sometimes I serve them over rice.

- 1/3 cup water
- 1/4 cup tomato paste
- 3 tablespoons brown sugar
- 1 tablespoon prepared mustard

Throw-Together Short Ribs

- 2 teaspoons seasoned salt
- 2 teaspoons cider vinegar
- 1 teaspoon Worcestershire sauce
- 1 teaspoon beef bouillon granules
- 2 pounds beef short ribs
- 1 small tomato, chopped
- 1 small onion, chopped
- 1 tablespoon cornstarch
- 1 tablespoon cold water

In a 3-qt. slow cooker, combine the first eight ingredients. Add the ribs, tomato and onion. Cover and cook on low for 4-5 hours or until meat is tender.

In a small bowl, combine cornstarch and cold water until smooth; gradually stir into cooking juices. Cover and cook for 10-15 minutes or until thickened. **Yield:** 4-5 servings.

Hearty Hash Brown Dinner

Cook Time: 4-1/2 to 5 Hours

Marge Berg, Gibbon, Minnesota

This meal-in-one is frequent fare at our house. The combination of beef, potatoes and cheese can't be beat.

- 3 cups frozen shredded hash brown potatoes, thawed
- 1/2 teaspoon salt
- 1/4 teaspoon pepper
- 1 pound ground beef
- 1/2 cup chopped onion
- 1 package (16 ounces) frozen California-blend vegetables
- 1 can (10-3/4 ounces) condensed cream of chicken soup, undiluted
- 1 cup milk
- 12 ounces process cheese (Velveeta), cubed
- 1 can (2.8 ounces) french-fried onions

Place the hash brown potatoes in a lightly greased 5-qt. slow cooker; sprinkle with salt and pepper. In a skillet, cook beef and onion over medium heat until the meat is no longer pink; drain. Spoon over the potatoes. Top with vegetables. Combine soup and milk; pour over vegetables. Cover and cook on low for 4 to 4-1/2 hours.

Top with cheese; cover and cook 30 minutes longer or until cheese is melted. Just before serving, sprinkle with french-fried onions. **Yield:** 4 servings.

Easy Chow Mein

(Pictured above right)

Cook Time: 4 Hours

Kay Bade, Mitchell, South Dakota

Our daughter welcomed me home from a hospital stay some years ago with this Asian dish and a copy of the recipe.

Easy Chow Mein

the soup, water, soup mix, pepper and garlic powder. Pour over the beef. Cover and cook on low for 6-8 hours or until meat and potatoes are tender. **Yield:** 4 servings.

Flavorful Pot Roast

(Pictured below)

Cook Time: 7 to 8 Hours

Arlene Butler, Ogden, Utah

I season this must-try pot roast with convenient envelopes of salad dressing and gravy mixes. It's easy! Sometimes I also thicken the flavorful cooking juices to create gravy and serve it over mashed potatoes.

> 2 boneless beef chuck roasts
> (2-1/2 pounds *each*)
> 1 envelope ranch salad dressing mix
> 1 envelope Italian salad dressing mix
> 1 envelope brown gravy mix
> 1/2 cup water

Place the chuck roasts in a 5-qt. slow cooker. In a small bowl, combine the salad dressing and gravy mixes; stir in water. Pour over meat. Cover and cook on low for 7-8 hours or until tender. If desired, thicken cooking juices for gravy. **Yield:** 12-15 servings.

> 1 pound ground beef
> 1 medium onion, chopped
> 1 bunch celery, sliced
> 2 cans (14 ounces *each*) Chinese vegetables, drained
> 2 envelopes brown gravy mix
> 2 tablespoons soy sauce
> Hot cooked rice

In a skillet, cook beef and onion over medium heat until meat is no longer pink; drain. Transfer to a slow cooker. Stir in the celery, Chinese vegetables, gravy mixes and soy sauce. Cover and cook on low for 4 hours or until celery is tender, stirring occasionally. Serve over rice. **Yield:** 8 servings.

Round Steak Supper

Cook Time: 6 to 8 Hours

Sandra Castillo, Janesville, Wisconsin

For this meat-and-potatoes dinner, round steak and potatoes are simmered for hours in an onion-flavored gravy.

> 4 large potatoes, peeled and cut into 1/2-inch cubes
> 1-1/2 pounds boneless beef round steak
> 1 can (10-3/4 ounces) condensed cream of mushroom soup, undiluted
> 1/2 cup water
> 1 envelope onion soup mix
> Pepper and garlic powder to taste

Place the potatoes in a slow cooker. Cut beef into four pieces; place over potatoes. In a bowl, combine

Flavorful Pot Roast

Slow-Cooked Coffee Beef Roast

Slow-Cooked Coffee Beef Roast

(Pictured above)

Cook Time: 8 to 10 Hours

Charles Trahan, San Dimas, California

Day-old coffee is the key to this flavorful beef roast that simmers in the slow cooker until it's fall-apart tender.

>   1 boneless beef sirloin tip roast
>   (2-1/2 pounds), cut in half
>   2 teaspoons canola oil
> 1-1/2 cups sliced fresh mushrooms
>   1/3 cup sliced green onions
>   2 garlic cloves, minced
> 1-1/2 cups brewed coffee
>   1 teaspoon Liquid Smoke, optional
>   1/2 teaspoon salt
>   1/2 teaspoon chili powder
>   1/4 teaspoon pepper
>   1/4 cup cornstarch
>   1/3 cup cold water

In a large nonstick skillet, brown roast over medium-high heat on all sides in oil. Place in a 5-qt. slow cooker. In the same skillet, saute mushrooms, onions and garlic until tender; stir in the coffee, Liquid Smoke if desired, salt, chili powder and pepper. Pour over roast. Cover and cook on low for 8-10 hours or until meat is tender.

Remove roast and keep warm. Pour cooking juices into a 2-cup measuring cup; skim fat. In a saucepan, combine cornstarch and water until smooth. Gradually stir in 2 cups cooking juices. Bring to a boil; cook and stir for 2 minutes or until thickened. Serve with sliced beef. **Yield:** 6 servings.

Beef Burgundy

Cook Time: 7-1/2 to 8-3/4 Hours

Sherri Mott, New Carlisle, Indiana

Savory cubes of beef are treated to a burgundy wine sauce and savory vegetables in this robust entree. It's wonderful over noodles or mashed potatoes.

>   6 bacon strips, diced
>   1 boneless beef chuck roast (3 pounds), cut
>   into 1-1/2-inch cubes
>   1 can (10-1/2 ounces) condensed beef broth,
>   undiluted
>   1 small onion, halved and sliced
>   1 medium carrot, sliced
>   2 tablespoons butter
>   1 tablespoon tomato paste
>   2 garlic cloves, minced
>   3/4 teaspoon dried thyme
>   1/2 teaspoon salt
>   1/2 teaspoon pepper
>   1 bay leaf
>   1/2 pound fresh mushrooms, sliced
>   1/2 cup burgundy wine *or* beef broth
>   5 tablespoons all-purpose flour
>   2/3 cup cold water
> Hot cooked noodles, optional

In a skillet, cook bacon over medium heat until crisp. Use a slotted spoon to remove to paper towels. In the drippings, brown the beef; drain. Place beef and bacon in a 5-qt. slow cooker. Add the broth, onion, carrot, butter, tomato paste, garlic, thyme, salt, pepper and bay leaf. Cover and cook on low for 7-8 hours or until meat is tender.

Add mushrooms and wine or broth. Combine flour and water until smooth; stir into slow cooker. Cover and cook on high for 30-45 minutes or until thickened. Discard bay leaf. Serve over noodles if desired. **Yield:** 8 servings.

Pizza Casserole

Cook Time: 1 Hour

Julie Sterchi, Harrisburg, Illinois

A friend from church gave me the recipe for this satisfying casserole. It's always one of the first dishes emptied at potlucks, and it can easily be adapted to personal tastes.

>   3 pounds ground beef
>   1/2 cup chopped onion
>   1 jar (28 ounces) spaghetti sauce
>   2 jars (4-1/2 ounces *each*) sliced mushrooms,
>   drained
>   1 teaspoon salt
>   1/2 teaspoon garlic powder
>   1/2 teaspoon dried oregano
> Dash pepper

1 package (16 ounces) wide egg noodles,
  cooked and drained
2 packages (3-1/2 ounces *each*) sliced pepperoni
2 cups (8 ounces) shredded cheddar cheese
2 cups (8 ounces) shredded part-skim
  mozzarella cheese

In a Dutch oven, brown beef and onion over medium heat until meat is no longer pink; drain. Add spaghetti sauce, mushrooms, salt, garlic powder, oregano and pepper; heat through. Spoon 4 cups into a 5-qt. slow cooker. Top with half of the noodles, pepperoni and cheeses. Repeat layers. Cover and cook on high for 1 hour or until cheese is melted. **Yield:** 12 servings.

Creamy Beef and Pasta

Cook Time: 6 Hours

Carol Losier, Baldwinsville, New York

A friend shared the recipe for this tasty meal. I often make it for our children when my husband and I go out.

2 cans (10-3/4 ounces *each*) condensed cream
  of mushroom soup, undiluted
2 cups (8 ounces) shredded cheddar *or*
  part-skim mozzarella cheese
1 pound ground beef, cooked and drained
2 cups uncooked small pasta
2 cups milk
1/2 to 1 teaspoon onion powder
1/2 to 1 teaspoon salt
1/4 to 1/2 teaspoon pepper

In a slow cooker, combine all ingredients; mix well. Cover and cook on low for 6 hours or until pasta is tender. **Yield:** 4-6 servings.

Confetti Casserole

Cook Time: 8 to 10 Hours

Joy Vincent, Newport, North Carolina

To create this comforting casserole, I adapted a recipe from the cookbook that came with my slow cooker.

1 pound ground beef
1 medium onion, finely chopped
1 teaspoon garlic powder
4 medium potatoes, peeled and quartered
3 medium carrots, cut into 1-inch chunks
1 package (10 ounces) frozen cut green beans
1 package (10 ounces) frozen corn
1 can (14-1/2 ounces) Italian diced tomatoes,
  undrained

In a skillet, cook beef, onion and garlic powder over medium heat until meat is no longer pink; drain. In a slow cooker, layer potatoes, carrots, beans and corn. Top with beef mixture. Pour tomatoes over the top. Cover and cook on low for 8-10 hours or until the potatoes are tender. **Yield:** 8 servings.

Old-World Sauerbraten

(Pictured below)

Cook Time: 6-1/4 to 8-1/4 Hours

Susan Garoutte, Georgetown, Texas

I serve this popular German entree with potato pancakes and vegetables. Crushed gingersnaps, lemon and cider vinegar give the beef its sweet-sour flavor.

1-1/2 cups water, *divided*
1-1/4 cups cider vinegar, *divided*
  2 large onions, sliced, *divided*
  1 medium lemon, sliced
 15 whole cloves, *divided*
  6 bay leaves, *divided*
  6 whole peppercorns
  2 tablespoons sugar
  2 teaspoons salt
  1 beef sirloin tip roast (3 pounds), cut in half
1/4 teaspoon pepper
 12 gingersnap cookies, crumbled

In a large resealable plastic bag, combine 1 cup water, 1 cup vinegar, half of the onions, lemon, 10 cloves, four bay leaves, peppercorns, sugar and salt; mix well. Add roast. Seal bag and turn to coat; refrigerate overnight, turning occasionally.

Drain and discard marinade. Place roast in a slow cooker; add pepper and remaining water, vinegar, onions, cloves and bay leaves. Cover and cook on low for 6-8 hours or until meat is tender. Remove roast and keep warm. Discard bay leaves. Stir in gingersnaps. Cover and cook on high for 10-15 minutes or until gravy is thickened. Slice roast; serve with gravy. **Yield:** 12 servings.

Old-World Sauerbraten

No-Fuss Swiss Steak

No-Fuss Swiss Steak

(Pictured above)

Cook Time: 6 to 8 Hours

Sharon Morrell, Parker, South Dakota

I make this main dish regularly because our children love the savory steak, tangy gravy and tender veggies.

- 3 pounds boneless beef round steak, cut into serving-size pieces
- 2 tablespoons vegetable oil
- 2 medium carrots, cut into 1/2-inch slices
- 2 celery ribs, cut into 1/2-inch slices
- 1-3/4 cups water
- 1 can (11 ounces) condensed tomato rice soup, undiluted
- 1 can (10-1/2 ounces) condensed French onion soup, undiluted
- 1/2 teaspoon pepper
- 1 bay leaf

In a large skillet, brown beef in oil over medium-high heat; drain. Transfer to a 5-qt. slow cooker. Add carrots and celery. Combine the remaining ingredients; pour over meat and vegetables. Cover and cook on low for 6-8 hours or until meat is tender. Discard the bay leaf before serving. Thicken cooking juices if desired. **Yield:** 8-10 servings.

Brisket with Cranberry Gravy

(Pictured at right)

Cook Time: 8 to 10 Hours

Nina Hall, Spokane, Wisconsin

Cranberry sauce adds sweetness to this no-stress take on brisket. Use jellied instead of whole-berry cranberry sauce if you like.

- 1 fresh beef brisket (2-1/2 pounds)
- 1/2 teaspoon salt
- 1/4 teaspoon pepper
- 1 can (16 ounces) whole-berry cranberry sauce
- 1 can (8 ounces) tomato sauce
- 1/2 cup chopped onion
- 1 tablespoon prepared mustard

Rub brisket with salt and pepper; place in a 5-qt. slow cooker. Combine the remaining ingredients; pour over brisket. Cover and cook on low for 8-10 hours or until meat is tender. Remove brisket; thinly slice across the grain. Skim fat from cooking juices; serve with brisket. **Yield:** 6-8 servings.

Melt-in-Your-Mouth Meat Loaf

Cook Time: 5-1/4 to 6-1/4 Hours

Suzanne Codner, Starbuck, Minnesota

My husband never liked meat loaf until I prepared this version. It instantly became his favorite meal.

- 2 eggs
- 3/4 cup milk
- 2/3 cup seasoned bread crumbs
- 2 teaspoons dried minced onion
- 1 teaspoon salt
- 1/2 teaspoon rubbed sage
- 1-1/2 pounds ground beef
- 1/4 cup ketchup
- 2 tablespoons brown sugar
- 1 teaspoon ground mustard
- 1/2 teaspoon Worcestershire sauce

In a large bowl, combine the first six ingredients. Crumble beef over mixture and mix well (mixture

Brisket with Cranberry Gravy

will be moist). Shape into a round loaf; place in a 5-qt. slow cooker. Cover and cook on low for 5-6 hours or until a meat thermometer reads 160°.

In a small bowl, whisk the ketchup, brown sugar, mustard and Worcestershire sauce. Spoon over the meat loaf. Cook 15 minutes longer or until heated through. Let stand for 10-15 minutes before cutting. **Yield:** 6 servings.

Hamburger Supper

(Pictured at right)

Cook Time: 4 to 6 Hours

Dolores Hickenbottom, Greensburg, Pennsylvania

My mother-in-law shared this classic meat-and-potatoes recipe with me. Over the years, I've relied on the hamburger dish more times than I can count. No one leaves the table hungry when this is on the menu.

- 1 **pound ground beef**
- 1/4 **cup hot water**
- 3 **small potatoes, peeled and diced**
- 1 **medium onion, chopped**
- 1 **can (15 ounces) peas and carrots, drained**
- 1 **can (14-1/2 ounces) diced tomatoes, undrained**
- 1 **tablespoon sugar**
- 1/2 **teaspoon salt**
- 1/4 **teaspoon pepper**

Shape beef into four patties. In a skillet, cook patties over medium heat until no longer pink. Transfer to a slow cooker. Add water to skillet and stir to loosen browned bits from pan. Pour into slow cooker. Add the remaining ingredients. Cover and cook on low for 4-6 hours or until potatoes are tender. **Yield:** 4 servings.

Colorful Veggie Medley

Cook Time: 4 Hours

Kerry Johnson, Decorah, Iowa

When my freezer or garden is bursting with vegetables, I bring out the slow cooker to prepare this dish. It makes good use of fresh-picked carrots, green pepper and more. With ground beef, it's also satisfying as a main course.

- 1-1/2 **pounds ground beef, cooked and drained**
- 1 **package (10 ounces) frozen cut green beans, thawed**
- 1 **package (10 ounces) frozen peas, thawed**
- 1 **package (6 ounces) frozen pea pods, thawed**
- 1 **can (14-1/2 ounces) diced tomatoes, undrained**
- 1-1/2 **cups thinly sliced carrots**
- 2 **celery ribs, sliced**

Hamburger Supper

- 1 **can (8 ounces) sliced water chestnuts, drained**
- 1/2 **cup chopped green pepper**
- 3 **tablespoons butter**
- 3 **tablespoons sugar**
- 3 **tablespoons quick-cooking tapioca**
- 1-1/2 **teaspoons salt**
- 1/2 **teaspoon pepper**

In a 5-qt. slow cooker, combine all of the ingredients and mix well. Cover and cook on low for 4 hours or until heated through. **Yield:** 6-8 servings.

Enchilada Casserole

Cook Time: 6 to 8 Hours

Denise Waller, Omaha, Nebraska

Tortilla chips and a side salad turn this casserole into a meal without much work.

- 1 **pound ground beef**
- 2 **cans (10 ounces *each*) enchilada sauce**
- 1 **can (10-3/4 ounces) condensed cream of onion soup, undiluted**
- 1/4 **teaspoon salt**
- 1 **package (8-1/2 ounces) flour tortillas, torn**
- 3 **cups (12 ounces) shredded cheddar cheese**

In a skillet, cook beef over medium heat until no longer pink; drain. Stir in the enchilada sauce, soup and salt. In a slow cooker, layer a third of the beef mixture, tortillas and cheese. Repeat the layers twice. Cover and cook on low for 6-8 hours or until heated through. **Yield:** 4 servings.

Meatball Tortellini

(Pictured above)

Cook Time: 3 to 4 Hours

Tracie Bergeron, Chauvin, Louisiana

I combined some filling staples from our freezer and pantry to come up with this easy-to-fix dish.

- 1 package (16 ounces) frozen California-blend vegetables, thawed
- 1 package (14 ounces) frozen cooked Italian meatballs, thawed
- 2 cups uncooked dried cheese tortellini
- 2 cans (10-3/4 ounces *each*) condensed cream of mushroom soup, undiluted
- 2-1/4 cups water
- 1 teaspoon Creole seasoning

In a 3-qt. slow cooker, combine the vegetables, meatballs and tortellini. In a large bowl, whisk the soup, water and Creole seasoning. Pour over vegetable-meatball mixture; stir well. Cover and cook on low for 3-4 hours or until the tortellini and vegetables are tender. **Yield:** 6-8 servings.

Editor's Note: The following spices may be substituted for the Creole seasoning—1/2 teaspoon *each* paprika and garlic powder, and a pinch *each* cayenne pepper, dried thyme and ground cumin.

Green Chili Beef Burritos

Cook Time: 8 to 9 Hours

Shirley Davidson, Thornton, Colorado

The meat is so tender in these beefy burritos. With plenty of seasonings, they truly spice up any meal.

- 2 boneless beef top sirloin roasts (3 pounds *each*)

- 4 cans (4 ounces *each*) chopped green chilies
- 1 medium onion, chopped
- 3 medium jalapeno peppers, seeded and chopped
- 3 garlic cloves, sliced
- 3 teaspoons chili powder
- 1-1/2 teaspoons ground cumin
- 1 teaspoon seasoning blend
- 1 cup beef broth
- 24 flour tortillas (7 inches), warmed
- Sliced tomatoes, shredded lettuce and cheddar cheese, optional

Trim fat from roasts; cut meat into large chunks. Place in a 5-qt. slow cooker. Top with chilies, onion, jalapenos, garlic, chili powder, cumin and seasoning blend. Pour broth over all. Cover and cook on low for 8-9 hours.

Remove beef; cool slightly. Shred with two forks. Cool cooking liquid slightly; skim fat. In a blender, cover and process cooking liquid in small batches until smooth. Return liquid and beef to slow cooker; heat through. Place 1/3 cup beef mixture on each tortilla. Top with lettuce, tomatoes and cheese if desired. Fold in ends and sides. **Yield:** 2 dozen.

Editor's Note: When cutting or seeding hot peppers, use rubber or plastic gloves to protect your hands. Avoid touching your face.

Sweet-and-Sour Pot Roast

(Pictured below)

Cook Time: 4 to 5 Hours

Erica Warkentin, Dundas, Ontario

I grew up on a farm, and we ate beef often. I was so pleased when I found this recipe more than 15 years ago, since it gives pot roast a new mouth-watering flavor.

Sweet-and-Sour Pot Roast

    12 small white potatoes, peeled
     1 boneless beef chuck roast (about 3 pounds)
     1 tablespoon vegetable oil
     1 cup chopped onion
     1 can (15 ounces) tomato sauce
   1/4 cup packed brown sugar
     2 to 3 tablespoons Worcestershire sauce
     2 tablespoons cider vinegar
     1 teaspoon salt

Place the potatoes in a slow cooker. Trim the fat from the roast; brown roast in hot oil on all sides in a skillet. Place the meat in the slow cooker. Discard all but 1 tablespoon drippings from skillet; saute onion until tender. Stir in tomato sauce, brown sugar, Worcestershire sauce, vinegar and salt. Pour over meat and potatoes.

Cover and cook on high for 4-5 hours or until the meat is tender. Before serving, pour sauce into a skillet. Cook and stir over medium-high heat until thickened; serve with potatoes and meat. **Yield:** 6-8 servings.

Moroccan Braised Beef

Moroccan Braised Beef

(Pictured at right)

Cook Time: 7 to 8 Hours

Curry powder, cumin, golden raisins and couscous help this out-of-the-ordinary beef dish from our Test Kitchen bring exotic flair to your dinner table. Try this recipe when you want to add a little spice to a weeknight supper or serve guests an impressive main course.

   1/3 cup all-purpose flour
     2 pounds boneless beef chuck roast, cut into
        1-inch cubes
     3 tablespoons olive oil
     2 cans (14-1/2 ounces *each*) beef broth
     2 cups chopped onions
     1 can (14-1/2 ounces) diced tomatoes,
        undrained
     1 cup dry red wine
     1 tablespoon curry powder
     1 tablespoon paprika
     1 teaspoon salt
     1 teaspoon ground cumin
     1 teaspoon ground coriander
   1/2 teaspoon cayenne pepper
1-1/2 cups golden raisins
Hot cooked couscous, optional

Place the flour in a large resealable plastic bag; add the beef and toss to coat. In a large skillet, brown the beef in oil. Transfer to a 5-qt. slow cooker. Stir in the broth, onions, tomatoes, wine and seasonings. Cover and cook on low for 7-8 hours or until the meat is tender.

During the last 30 minutes of cooking, stir in the golden raisins. Serve with couscous if desired. **Yield:** 6 servings.

Two-Step Stroganoff

Cook Time: 7 Hours

Roberta Menefee, Walcott, New York

I like to make this slow-cooked dinner on hot summer days when I want to keep my kitchen cool.

     2 pounds ground beef, cooked and drained
     2 medium onions, chopped
     1 cup beef consomme
     1 can (4 ounces) mushroom stems and pieces,
        drained
     3 tablespoons tomato paste
     2 garlic cloves, minced
1-1/2 teaspoons salt
   1/4 teaspoon pepper
     2 tablespoons all-purpose flour
   3/4 cup sour cream
Hot cooked noodles

In a slow cooker, combine the first eight ingredients; mix well. Cover and cook on low for 6 hours. In a small bowl, combine flour and sour cream until smooth; stir into beef mixture. Cover and cook 1 hour longer or until thickened. Serve over noodles. **Yield:** 6 servings.

Fix a Future Meal

Moroccan Braised Beef (recipe at left) can be prepared and frozen for future use. Be sure to store it in an airtight container and use it within 2 months. When you're ready to eat, simply thaw this dish and reheat it.

Beef in Onion Gravy

(Pictured below)

Cook Time: 6 to 8 Hours

Denise Albers, Freeburg, Illinois

To feed our family of four, I double this home-style beef recipe and make plenty of noodles or mashed potatoes to go with it. My husband is always happy when we end up with leftovers because I send the extras along with him to work for lunch. His coworkers tell him he's lucky.

- 1 **can (10-3/4 ounces) condensed cream of mushroom soup, undiluted**
- 2 **tablespoons onion soup mix**
- 2 **tablespoons beef broth**
- 1 **tablespoon quick-cooking tapioca**
- 1 **pound beef stew meat, cut into 1-inch cubes**

Hot cooked noodles *or* mashed potatoes

In a slow cooker, combine the cream of mushroom soup, soup mix, beef broth and tapioca; let stand for 15 minutes. Stir in the beef.

Cover and cook on low for 6-8 hours or until the meat is tender. Serve over noodles or mashed potatoes. **Yield:** 3 servings.

Hearty Wild Rice

Cook Time: 5 Hours

Mrs. Garnet Pettigrew, Columbia City, Indiana

My father-in-law used to make this casserole in the oven, and and I adapted the recipe for the slow cooker so I wouldn't need to keep an eye on it.

- 1 **pound ground beef**
- 1/2 **pound bulk pork sausage**
- 6 **celery ribs, diced**
- 2 **cans (10-1/2 ounces *each*) condensed beef broth, undiluted**
- 1-1/4 **cups water**
- 1 **medium onion, chopped**
- 1 **cup uncooked wild rice**
- 1 **can (4 ounces) mushroom stems and pieces, drained**
- 1/4 **cup soy sauce**

In a skillet, cook beef and sausage over medium heat until no longer pink; drain. Transfer to a 5-qt. slow cooker. Add the celery, broth, water, onion, rice, mushrooms and soy sauce; mix well.

Cover and cook on high for 1 hour. Reduce heat to low; cover and cook for 4 hours or until the rice is tender. **Yield:** 10-12 servings.

Beef in Onion Gravy

Corned Beef 'n' Cabbage

(Pictured at right)

Cook Time: 8 to 10 Hours

Jo Ann Honey, Longmont, Colorado

I have Irish ancestry, so a few years ago I started a tradition of making this delicious, slow-cooked meal on St. Patrick's Day.

- 1 large onion, cut into wedges
- 1 cup apple juice
- 1 bay leaf
- 1 corned beef brisket with spice packet (2-1/2 to 3 pounds), cut in half
- 1 small head cabbage, cut into wedges

Place the onion in a 5-qt. slow cooker. Combine the apple juice, bay leaf and contents of spice packet; pour over onion. Top with brisket and cabbage. Cover and cook on low for 8-10 hours or until meat and vegetables are tender. Discard bay leaf before serving. **Yield:** 6 servings.

Egg Noodle Lasagna

Cook Time: 4 Hours

Mary Oberlin, Selinsgrove, Pennsylvania

The perfect take-along for charity events and church potluck suppers, this comforting crowd-pleaser is sure to satisfy everyone in attendance.

- 6-1/2 cups uncooked wide egg noodles
- 3 tablespoons butter
- 1-1/2 pounds ground beef
- 2-1/4 cups spaghetti sauce
- 6 ounces process cheese (Velveeta), cubed
- 3 cups (12 ounces) shredded part-skim mozzarella cheese

Cook noodles according to package directions; drain. Add butter and toss to coat. In a skillet, cook beef over medium heat until no longer pink; drain. Spread a fourth of the spaghetti sauce in an ungreased 5-qt. slow cooker. Layer with a third of the noodles, a third of the beef, a third of the remaining sauce and a third of the cheeses. Repeat layers twice.

Cover and cook on low for 4 hours or until cheese is melted and lasagna is heated through. **Yield:** 12-16 servings.

Two-Pot Dinner

Cook Time: 4 Hours

Jean Roper, Palermo, California

My daughter received this side dish recipe from a friend a while ago. Bacon gives it a wonderfully rich flavor, making it a fa-

Corned Beef 'n' Cabbage

vorite dish to pass. It's perfect to set on a barbecue buffet in the summertime. Try it the next time you're serving hamburgers or hot dogs from the grill.

- 1 pound sliced bacon, cut into 2-inch pieces
- 1 large onion, chopped
- 1 pound ground beef
- 1 can (31 ounces) pork and beans
- 1 can (30 ounces) kidney beans, rinsed and drained
- 1 can (15 ounces) great northern beans, rinsed and drained
- 1 cup ketchup
- 1/3 cup packed brown sugar
- 3 tablespoons vinegar
- 1 tablespoon Liquid Smoke, optional

In a skillet, cook bacon over medium heat until crisp; remove with a slotted spoon to a slow cooker. Reserve 2 tablespoons drippings in the pan. Saute onion in drippings until browned; remove with a slotted spoon to slow cooker. In the same skillet, cook beef until no longer pink; drain and transfer to slow cooker. Add the remaining ingredients; mix well. Cover and cook on low for 4 hours or until heated through. **Yield:** 10 servings.

Chicken & Turkey

Spicy Lemon Chicken (p. 68)

Chapter 5

Sunday Chicken Supper for Two

(Pictured below)

Cook Time: 6 to 8 Hours

Ruthann Martin, Louisville, Ohio

This is a pared-down version of a recipe that has a larger yield. With two pieces of chicken and vegetables, it's a complete dinner that's nice for Sunday or any day of the week.

    2 small carrots, cut into 2-inch pieces
  1/2 medium onion, chopped
  1/2 celery rib, cut into 2-inch pieces
    1 cup cut fresh green beans
      (2-inch pieces)
    2 small red potatoes, halved
    2 bone-in chicken breast halves
      (7 ounces *each*), skin removed
    2 bacon strips, cooked and crumbled
  3/4 cup hot water
    1 teaspoon chicken bouillon granules
  1/4 teaspoon salt
  1/4 teaspoon dried thyme
  1/4 teaspoon dried basil
Pinch pepper

In a 3-qt. slow cooker, layer the first seven ingredients in order listed. In a bowl, combine the remaining ingredients; pour over the top. Do not stir. Cover and cook on low for 6-8 hours or until vegetables are tender and chicken juices run clear.

Remove chicken and vegetables. Thicken cooking juices for gravy if desired. **Yield:** 2 servings.

Sunday Chicken Supper for Two

Chicken with Stuffing

Cook Time: 4 Hours

Susan Kutz, Stillman Valley, Illinois

Only five ingredients are needed for this comforting home-style chicken so it's ideal for days when I don't have time to search my pantry for a number of different items. Topped with corn bread stuffing from a convenient mix, it's a satisfying meal that cooks on its own while I tend to other things.

    4 boneless skinless chicken breast halves
    1 can (10-3/4 ounces) condensed cream of
      chicken soup, undiluted
1-1/4 cups water
  1/4 cup butter, melted
    1 package (6 ounces) corn bread stuffing mix

Place chicken in a greased slow cooker. Top with soup. In a bowl, combine the water, butter and stuffing mix; spoon over the chicken. Cover and cook on low for 4 hours or until chicken juices run clear. **Yield:** 4 servings.

Mushroom Chicken Cacciatore

Cook Time: 4 to 5 Hours

Jane Bone, Cape Coral, Florida

I give an Italian treatment to chicken breasts by slow cooking them in a zesty tomato sauce and then serving them over spaghetti. My dinner guests are often surprised that such a special entree was prepared in the slow cooker. I'm always happy to share the recipe.

    4 boneless skinless chicken breast halves
      (about 1-1/2 pounds)
    2 tablespoons vegetable oil
    1 can (15 ounces) tomato sauce
    2 cans (4 ounces *each*) sliced mushrooms,
      drained
    1 medium onion, chopped
  1/4 cup red wine *or* chicken broth
    2 garlic cloves, minced
1-1/4 teaspoons dried oregano
  1/2 teaspoon dried thyme
  1/8 to 1/4 teaspoon salt
  1/8 teaspoon pepper
Hot cooked spaghetti

In a large skillet, brown chicken in oil on both sides. Transfer to a slow cooker. In a bowl, combine the tomato sauce, mushrooms, onion, wine or broth, garlic, oregano, thyme, salt and pepper; pour over chicken. Cover and cook on low for 4-5 hours or until chicken juices run clear. Serve over spaghetti. **Yield:** 4 servings.

Corsican Chicken

er and cook on low for 4-5 hours or until chicken juices run clear. Add the olives and orange peel. Cover and cook on high for 30 minutes. Remove chicken and keep warm.

Pour cooking juices into a small saucepan; skim fat. Combine cornstarch and water until smooth; gradually stir into cooking juices. Bring to a boil; cook and stir for 2 minutes or until smooth. Pour over chicken. Sprinkle with basil, pimientos and parsley. **Yield:** 6-8 servings.

Corsican Chicken

(Pictured above)

Cook Time: 4-1/2 to 5-1/2 Hours

Mary Bergfeld, Eugene, Oregon

These moist chicken thighs make a delicious, heartwarming entree for winter months—just add a salad and dessert.

    3 tablespoons butter, softened
    2 tablespoons herbes de Provence
    1 teaspoon salt
    2 garlic cloves, minced
  1/2 teaspoon coarsely ground pepper
    2 pounds boneless skinless chicken thighs
    1 large onion, chopped
  1/2 cup oil-packed sun-dried tomatoes,
       julienned
    1 can (10-1/2 ounces) condensed beef
       consomme, undiluted
  1/2 cup dry vermouth *or* orange juice
  1/2 cup pitted Greek olives, quartered
    1 teaspoon grated orange peel
    2 teaspoons cornstarch
    1 tablespoon cold water
    2 tablespoons minced fresh basil
    2 tablespoons diced pimientos
    2 tablespoons minced fresh parsley

In a small bowl, combine the butter, herbes de Provence, salt, garlic and pepper; rub over chicken. Place in a 5-qt. slow cooker. Add the onion, tomatoes, consomme and vermouth or orange juice. Cov-

Turkey Thigh Supper

(Pictured below)

Cook Time: 7 to 8 Hours

Betty Gingrich, Oxford, Arkansas

This family-pleasing meal-in-one has it all—tender turkey thighs, tasty vegetables and a homemade sauce. I like to cook chicken breasts the same way.

    3 medium red potatoes, cut into chunks
  1/2 pound fresh baby carrots
    2 medium onions, cut into chunks
    4 turkey thighs, skin removed
    1 can (10-3/4 ounces) condensed tomato
       soup, undiluted
  1/3 cup water
    1 teaspoon minced garlic
    1 teaspoon Italian seasoning
  1/2 to 1 teaspoon salt

In a 5-qt. slow cooker, layer the potatoes, carrots and onions. Top with turkey. Combine soup, water, garlic, Italian seasoning and salt; pour over turkey. Cover and cook on high for 7-8 hours or until a meat thermometer reads 170° and vegetables are tender. **Yield:** 4 servings.

Turkey Thigh Supper

Hearty Chicken Enchiladas

Hearty Chicken Enchiladas

(Pictured above)

Cook Time: 8 Hours

Jenny Miller, Raleigh, North Carolina

My husband, Nathan, and I really like Mexican food, and this is our favorite dish. You can modify it to suit your taste, adding corn, rice or even refried beans.

> 1 **pound boneless skinless chicken breasts**
> 2 **cans (15 ounces *each*) enchilada sauce**
> 1 **can (4 ounces) chopped green chilies**
> 1 **can (15 ounces) black beans, rinsed and drained**
> 8 **flour tortillas (6 inches)**
> 1 **cup (4 ounces) shredded Mexican cheese blend**
> **Sour cream, optional**

In a 3-qt. slow cooker, combine the chicken, enchilada sauce and chilies. Cover and cook on low for 8 hours or until a meat thermometer reads 160°.

Remove chicken and shred with two forks. Reserve 1-2/3 cups cooking juices. Pour the remaining cooking juices into a large bowl; add the beans and shredded chicken. Coat two freezer-safe 8-in. square baking dishes with nonstick cooking spray; add 1/2 cup reserved juices to each.

Place about 1/3 cup chicken mixture down the center of each tortilla. Roll up and place seam side down in prepared dishes. Pour remaining reserved juices over top; sprinkle with cheese.

Cover and freeze one dish for up to 3 months. Cover and bake the second dish at 350° for 20 minutes. Uncover; bake 5 minutes longer or until cheese

is lightly browned. Serve with sour cream if desired. **Yield:** 4 servings.

To use frozen enchiladas: Thaw in the refrigerator overnight. Remove from the refrigerator 30 minutes before baking. Bake as directed.

Sage Turkey Thighs

(Pictured below)

Cook Time: 6 to 8 Hours

Natalie Swanson, Catonsville, Maryland

I created this for my boys, who love dark meat. It's like our traditional Thanksgiving turkey that's seasoned with sage.

> 4 **medium carrots, halved**
> 1 **medium onion, chopped**
> 1/2 **cup water**
> 2 **garlic cloves, minced**
> 1-1/2 **teaspoons rubbed sage, *divided***
> 2 **turkey thighs *or* drumsticks (about 2 pounds), skin removed**
> 1 **teaspoon browning sauce, optional**
> 1/4 **teaspoon salt**
> 1/8 **teaspoon pepper**
> 1 **tablespoon cornstarch**
> 1/4 **cup cold water**

In a slow cooker, combine the carrots, onion, water, garlic and 1 teaspoon sage. Top with the turkey thighs. Sprinkle with the remaining sage. Cover and cook on low for 6-8 hours or until a meat thermometer reads 180°.

Remove turkey and keep warm. Skim fat from cooking juices; strain and reserve vegetables. Place vegetables in a food processor; cover and process until smooth. Place in a saucepan; add cooking

Sage Turkey Thighs

juices. Bring to a boil. Add browning sauce if desired, salt and pepper. Combine cornstarch and water until smooth; add to juices. Bring to a boil; cook and stir for 2 minutes or until thickened. Serve with the turkey. **Yield:** 4 servings.

Slow-Cooked Herbed Turkey

Cook Time: 3-1/2 to 4 Hours

Sue A. Jurack, Mequon, Wisconsin

When herbs are plentiful in my garden, I prepare this recipe. The turkey stays moist and is bursting with flavor.

 1 can (14-1/2 ounces) chicken broth
 1/2 cup lemon juice
 1/4 cup packed brown sugar
 1/4 cup minced fresh sage
 1/4 cup minced fresh thyme
 1/4 cup lime juice
 1/4 cup cider vinegar
 1/4 cup olive oil
 1 envelope onion soup mix
 2 tablespoons Dijon mustard
 1 tablespoon minced fresh marjoram
 1-1/2 teaspoons paprika
 1 teaspoon garlic powder
 1 teaspoon pepper
 1/2 teaspoon salt
 2 boneless turkey breasts (2 pounds *each*)

In a blender, combine the first 15 ingredients; cover and process until blended. Place the turkey breasts in a gallon-size resealable plastic bag; add marinade. Seal bag and turn to coat; seal and refrigerate overnight.

Transfer turkey breasts to a 5-qt. slow cooker. Pour marinade into a large saucepan; bring to a rolling boil for 1 minute. Pour over turkey. Cover and cook on high for 3-1/2 to 4 hours or until juices run clear and a meat thermometer reads 170°. Let stand for 10 minutes before slicing. **Yield:** 14-16 servings.

Southern Barbecue Spaghetti Sauce

(Pictured above right)

Cook Time: 4 to 5 Hours

Rhonda Melanson, Sarnia, Ontario

I revamped our favorite sloppy joe recipe into this thick spaghetti sauce that simmers in the slow cooker. The flavor is jazzy yet mild enough to be enjoyed by children.

 1 pound lean ground turkey
 2 medium onions, chopped
 1-1/2 cups sliced fresh mushrooms
 1 medium green pepper, chopped

Southern Barbecue Spaghetti Sauce

 2 garlic cloves, minced
 1 can (14-1/2 ounces) diced tomatoes, undrained
 1 can (12 ounces) tomato paste
 1 can (8 ounces) tomato sauce
 1 cup ketchup
 1/2 cup beef broth
 2 tablespoons Worcestershire sauce
 2 tablespoons brown sugar
 1 tablespoon ground cumin
 2 teaspoons chili powder
 12 cups hot cooked spaghetti

In a large nonstick skillet, cook the turkey, onions, mushrooms, green pepper and garlic over medium heat until meat is no longer pink; drain. Transfer to a slow cooker. Stir in the tomatoes, tomato paste, tomato sauce, ketchup, broth, Worcestershire sauce, brown sugar, cumin and chili powder; mix well.

Cover and cook on low for 4-5 hours. Serve over spaghetti. **Yield:** 12 servings.

Take It Easy on Turkey Day

This Thanksgiving, why not branch out from the traditional roasted turkey? With Slow-Cooked Herbed Turkey (recipe above left), you can prepare a delicious, family-pleasing dinner with a minimum of fuss.

You'll get a head start on your holiday feast by whipping up the flavorful marinade the evening before and then marinating the turkey breasts overnight. On the day of the meal, all you'll have left to do is boil the marinade in a saucepan. The slow cooker will do the remaining work, and you can turn your attention to preparing the rest of your menu.

Sweet-and-Sour Chicken

(Pictured below and on front cover)

Cook Time: 3-1/2 Hours

Dorothy Hess, Hartwell, Georgia

Adding the pineapple and peas later in the process keeps them from becoming overcooked in this stir-fry-like supper.

1-1/4 **pounds boneless skinless chicken breasts, cut into 1-inch strips**
   1 **tablespoon vegetable oil**
Salt and pepper to taste
   1 **can (8 ounces) pineapple chunks**
   1 **can (8 ounces) sliced water chestnuts, drained**
   2 **medium carrots, sliced**
   2 **tablespoons soy sauce**
   4 **teaspoons cornstarch**
   1 **cup sweet-and-sour sauce**
 1/4 **cup water**
1-1/2 **teaspoons ground ginger**
   3 **green onions, cut into 1-inch pieces**
1-1/2 **cups fresh *or* frozen snow peas**
Hot cooked rice

In a large skillet, saute chicken in oil for 4-5 minutes; drain. Sprinkle with salt and pepper. Drain pineapple, reserving juice; set pineapple aside. In a 5-qt. slow cooker, combine the chicken, water chestnuts, carrots, soy sauce and pineapple juice. Cover and cook on low for 3 hours.

In a small bowl, combine the cornstarch, sweet-and-sour sauce, water and ginger until smooth. Stir into the slow cooker. Add onions and pineapple; cover and cook on high for 15 minutes or until thickened. Add peas; cook 5 minutes longer. Serve with rice. **Yield:** 5 servings.

Chicken in Sour Cream Sauce

Cook Time: 6 to 8 Hours

Jane Carlovsky, Sebring, Florida

Great for family or guests, this bone-in chicken is dressed up in a flavorful cream sauce with fresh mushrooms.

1-1/2 **teaspoons salt**
 1/4 **teaspoon pepper**
 1/4 **teaspoon paprika**
 1/4 **teaspoon lemon-pepper seasoning**
   6 **bone-in chicken breast halves, skin removed**
   1 **can (10-3/4 ounces) condensed cream of mushroom soup, undiluted**
   1 **cup (8 ounces) sour cream**
 1/2 **cup dry white wine *or* chicken broth**
 1/2 **pound fresh mushrooms, sliced**

Combine the first four ingredients; rub over chicken. Place in a slow cooker. In a bowl, combine the soup, sour cream, and wine or broth; stir in mushrooms. Pour over chicken. Cover and cook on low for 6-8 hours or until chicken juices run clear. Thicken the sauce if desired. **Yield:** 6 servings.

Sweet-and-Sour Chicken

Creamy Herbed Chicken

Cook Time: 4 to 5 Hours

Mary Humeniuk-Smith, Perry Hall, Maryland

I work nights, so when I get home in the morning, I put this chicken on to cook. When I'm ready to eat, the juicy chicken and well-seasoned sauce are delicious.

    4 boneless skinless chicken breast halves
    1 can (10-3/4 ounces) condensed cream of
      chicken soup, undiluted
    1 cup milk
    1 envelope garlic and herb pasta sauce mix
    1 teaspoon dried thyme
    1 teaspoon dried parsley flakes
Hot cooked fettuccine

Place chicken in a slow cooker. Combine the soup, milk, sauce mix, thyme and parsley; pour over chicken. Cover and cook on low for 4-5 hours or until chicken juices run clear. Serve over fettuccine. **Yield:** 4 servings.

Editor's Note: This recipe was tested with Knorr Garlic Herb Pasta Sauce Mix.

Slow-Cooked Italian Chicken

Cook Time: 4 to 5 Hours

Deanna D'Auria, Banning, California

With tomatoes, green pepper and garlic, this enticing chicken entree is especially good over pasta or rice.

    4 boneless skinless chicken breast halves
      (4 ounces *each*)
    1 can (14-1/2 ounces) chicken broth
    1 can (14-1/2 ounces) stewed tomatoes, cut up
    1 can (8 ounces) tomato sauce
    1 medium green pepper, chopped
    1 green onion, chopped
    1 garlic clove, minced
    3 teaspoons chili powder
    1 teaspoon ground mustard
  1/2 teaspoon garlic salt *or* garlic powder
  1/2 teaspoon onion salt *or* onion powder
  1/2 teaspoon pepper
  1/3 cup all-purpose flour
  1/2 cup cold water
Hot cooked noodles

Place the chicken in a slow cooker. In a bowl, combine the next 11 ingredients; pour over chicken. Cover and cook on low for 4-5 hours or until chicken juices run clear.

Remove chicken and keep warm. Pour cooking juices into a saucepan; skim fat. Combine flour and cold water until smooth; stir into juices. Bring to a boil; cook and stir for 2 minutes or until thickened. Serve over chicken and noodles. **Yield:** 4 servings.

Chicken with Vegetables

Chicken with Vegetables

(Pictured above)

Cook Time: 5 Hours

Norlene Razak, Kyle, Texas

This main course comes together so easily. It's simple, tasty and a great way to get your family to eat their vegetables.

    1 cup sliced fresh mushrooms
    4 chicken legs, skin removed
    4 chicken thighs, skin removed
    4 celery ribs, sliced
    1 cup sliced zucchini
    1 cup sliced carrots
    1 medium onion, sliced
    1 cup tomato juice
  1/2 cup chicken broth
    1 garlic clove, minced
  1/4 teaspoon paprika
Pepper to taste
    3 tablespoons cornstarch
    3 tablespoons cold water
Hot cooked rice

Place mushrooms and chicken in a slow cooker. Add the celery, zucchini, carrots, onion, tomato juice, broth, garlic, paprika and pepper. Cover and cook on low for 5 hours or until meat juices run clear.

Remove chicken and vegetables and keep warm. Transfer cooking juices to a saucepan; skim fat. Combine the cornstarch and water until smooth; add to the juices. Bring to a boil; cook and stir for 2 minutes or until thickened. Pour over chicken and vegetables; serve over rice. **Yield:** 4 servings.

Spicy Lemon Chicken

Spicy Lemon Chicken

(Pictured above and on page 60)

Cook Time: 4 to 5 Hours

Nancy Rambo, Riverside, California

I modified this recipe to work in our slow cooker. We enjoy the lemony chicken with rice or buttered noodles.

    1 medium onion, chopped
1/3 cup water
1/4 cup lemon juice
    1 tablespoon vegetable oil
1/2 to 1 teaspoon salt
1/2 teaspoon *each* garlic powder, chili powder
      and paprika
1/2 teaspoon ground ginger
1/4 teaspoon pepper
    4 boneless skinless chicken breast halves
      (4 ounces *each*)
4-1/2 teaspoons cornstarch
4-1/2 teaspoons cold water
Hot cooked noodles
Chopped fresh parsley, optional

In a greased slow cooker, combine the onion, water, lemon juice, oil and seasonings. Add chicken; turn to coat. Cover and cook on low for 4-5 hours or until a meat thermometer reads 170°. Remove chicken and keep warm.

   In a saucepan, combine the cornstarch and cold water until smooth. Gradually add the cooking juices. Bring to a boil; cook and stir for 2 minutes or until thickened. Serve with chicken over noodles. Sprinkle with parsley if desired. **Yield:** 4 servings.

Tangy Barbecue Wings

(Pictured below)

Cook Time: 3 to 4 Hours

Sherry Pitzer, Troy, Michigan

When I took these savory, slow-cooked appetizers to work, they were gone before I even got a bite! The tangy sauce makes the wings lip-smacking good.

  25 whole chicken wings (about 5 pounds)
2-1/2 cups hot and spicy ketchup
  2/3 cup white vinegar
  1/2 cup plus 2 tablespoons honey
  1/2 cup molasses
    1 teaspoon salt
    1 teaspoon Worcestershire sauce
  1/2 teaspoon onion powder
  1/2 teaspoon chili powder
  1/2 to 1 teaspoon Liquid Smoke, optional

Cut chicken wings into three sections and discard wing tip section. Place chicken wings in two greased 15-in. x 10-in. x 1-in. baking pans. Bake, uncovered, at 375° for 30 minutes; drain. Turn wings; bake 20-25 minutes longer or until juices run clear. Meanwhile, in a large saucepan, combine the remaining ingredients. Bring to a boil. Reduce heat; simmer, uncovered, for 25-30 minutes.

   Drain wings; place a third of them in a 5-qt. slow cooker. Top with about 1 cup sauce. Repeat layers twice. Cover and cook on low for 3-4 hours. Stir before serving. **Yield:** about 4 dozen.

   Editor's Note: 5 pounds of uncooked chicken wing sections (wingettes) may be substituted for the whole chicken wings. Omit the first step.

Tangy Barbecue Wings

Tarragon Mushroom Chicken

Cook Time: 4 to 5 Hours

Mary Kretschmer, Miami, Florida

I make this tasty dish when my grandchildren visit. Using the slow cooker leaves me time to enjoy their company.

- 6 boneless skinless chicken breast halves (4 ounces *each*)
- 1 can (10-3/4 ounces) condensed cream of chicken soup, undiluted
- 1 jar (4-1/2 ounces) sliced mushrooms, drained
- 1/2 cup sherry *or* chicken broth
- 2 tablespoons butter, melted
- 1 teaspoon dried tarragon
- 1 teaspoon Worcestershire sauce
- 1/4 teaspoon garlic powder
- 1/4 cup all-purpose flour

Place the chicken in a 5-qt. slow cooker. In a small bowl, combine the soup, mushrooms, sherry or broth, butter, tarragon, Worcestershire sauce and garlic powder; pour over chicken. Cover and cook on low for 4-5 hours or until chicken juices run clear.

Remove chicken and keep warm. Place the flour in a small saucepan; gradually whisk in cooking liquid until blended. Bring to a boil; cook and stir for 2 minutes or until thickened. Serve over chicken. **Yield:** 6 servings.

Citrus Turkey Roast

(Pictured above right)

Cook Time: 5 to 6 Hours

Kathy Kittell, Lenexa, Kansas

I was skeptical at first about fixing turkey in a slow cooker, but once I tasted this dish, I was hooked.

- 1 frozen boneless turkey roast (3 pounds), thawed
- 1 tablespoon garlic powder
- 1 tablespoon paprika
- 1 tablespoon olive oil
- 2 teaspoons Worcestershire sauce
- 1/2 teaspoon salt
- 1/2 teaspoon pepper
- 8 garlic cloves, peeled
- 1 cup chicken broth, *divided*
- 1/4 cup water
- 1/4 cup white wine *or* additional chicken broth
- 1/4 cup orange juice
- 1 tablespoon lemon juice
- 2 tablespoons cornstarch

Cut roast in half. Combine the garlic powder, paprika, oil, Worcestershire sauce, salt and pepper; rub over turkey. Place in a 5-qt. slow cooker. Add the

Citrus Turkey Roast

garlic, 1/2 cup broth, water, wine or additional broth, orange juice and lemon juice. Cover and cook on low for 5-6 hours or until a meat thermometer reads 170°.

Remove turkey and keep warm. Discard garlic cloves. For gravy, combine cornstarch and remaining broth until smooth; stir into cooking juices. Cover and cook on high for 15 minutes or until thickened. Slice turkey and serve with gravy. **Yield:** 12 servings.

Lemonade Chicken

Cook Time: 3 Hours

Jenny Cook, Eau Claire, Wisconsin

I don't know where this recipe originally came from, but my mother used to prepare it for our family when I was little, and now I love to make it.

- 6 boneless skinless chicken breast halves (4 ounces *each*)
- 3/4 cup lemonade concentrate
- 3 tablespoons ketchup
- 2 tablespoons brown sugar
- 1 tablespoon cider vinegar
- 2 tablespoons cornstarch
- 2 tablespoons cold water

Place chicken in a 5-qt. slow cooker. Combine the lemonade, ketchup, brown sugar and vinegar; pour over chicken. Cover and cook on low for 2-1/2 hours or until chicken juices run clear.

Remove chicken and keep warm. For gravy, combine cornstarch and water until smooth; stir into cooking juices. Cover and cook on high for 30 minutes or until thickened. Return chicken to the slow cooker; heat through. **Yield:** 6 servings.

Southwestern Chicken

Cook Time: 3 to 4 Hours

Karen Waters, Laurel, Maryland

Prepared salsa and convenient canned corn and beans add fun color, texture and flavor to this kid-pleasing dinner.

- 2 cans (15-1/4 ounces *each*) whole kernel corn, drained
- 1 can (15 ounces) black beans, rinsed and drained
- 1 jar (16 ounces) chunky salsa, *divided*
- 6 boneless skinless chicken breast halves
- 1 cup (4 ounces) shredded cheddar cheese

Combine the corn, black beans and 1/2 cup of salsa in a slow cooker. Top with chicken; pour the remaining salsa over chicken. Cover and cook on high for 3-4 hours or on low for 7-8 hours or until meat juices run clear. Sprinkle with cheese; cover until cheese is melted, about 5 minutes. **Yield:** 6 servings.

Sweet Pepper Chicken

(Pictured below)

Cook Time: 4 to 5 Hours

Ann Johnson, Dunn, North Carolina

Red and green peppers add attractive flair to this delightful chicken dish. Put it in the slow cooker before getting ready for church on Sunday morning. It'll be ready for you and your family to enjoy by the time you get home.

- 6 bone-in chicken breast halves, skin removed
- 1 tablespoon vegetable oil
- 2 cups sliced fresh mushrooms
- 1 medium onion, halved and sliced
- 1 medium green pepper, julienned
- 1 medium sweet red pepper, julienned
- 1 can (10-3/4 ounces) condensed cream of chicken soup, undiluted
- 1 can (10-3/4 ounces) condensed cream of mushroom soup, undiluted

Hot cooked rice

In a large skillet, brown chicken in oil on both sides. Transfer to a 5-qt. slow cooker. Top with mushrooms, onion and peppers. Combine the soups; pour over vegetables. Cover and cook on low for 4-5 hours or until chicken juices run clear. Serve with rice. **Yield:** 6 servings.

Turkey in a Pot

(Pictured above right)

Cook Time: 5 to 6 Hours

Lois Woodward, Okeechobee, Florida

This turkey breast gets a "holiday treatment"—thanks to the cranberry gravy seasoned with cinnamon, cloves and allspice.

- 1 boneless turkey breast (3 to 4 pounds), halved
- 1 can (16 ounces) whole-berry cranberry sauce
- 1/2 cup sugar

Sweet Pepper Chicken

Turkey in a Pot

1/2 cup apple juice
1 tablespoon cider vinegar
2 garlic cloves, minced
1 teaspoon ground mustard
1/2 teaspoon ground cinnamon
1/4 teaspoon ground cloves
1/4 teaspoon ground allspice
2 tablespoons all-purpose flour
1/4 cup cold water
1/4 teaspoon browning sauce, optional

Place the turkey skin side up in a 5-qt. slow cooker. Combine the cranberry sauce, sugar, apple juice, vinegar, garlic, mustard, cinnamon, cloves and allspice; pour over turkey. Cover and cook on low for 5-6 hours or until a meat thermometer reads 170°.

Remove turkey to a cutting board; keep warm. Strain cooking juices. In a saucepan, combine flour and water until smooth; gradually stir in strained juices. Bring to a boil; cook and stir for 2 minutes or until thickened. Stir in browning sauce if desired. Serve with sliced turkey. **Yield:** 12-16 servings.

Chicken Saltimbocca

Cook Time: 4 to 5 Hours

Carol McCollough, Missoula, Montana

White wine dresses up cream of chicken soup to make a lovely sauce for these chicken, ham and cheese roll-ups.

6 boneless skinless chicken breast halves
6 thin slices deli ham
6 slices Swiss cheese
1/4 cup all-purpose flour
1/4 cup grated Parmesan cheese
1/2 teaspoon salt
1/4 teaspoon pepper
2 tablespoons vegetable oil
1 can (10-3/4 ounces) condensed cream of chicken soup, undiluted
1/2 cup dry white wine *or* chicken broth
Hot cooked rice

Flatten chicken to 1/4-in. thickness. Top each piece with a slice of ham and cheese. Roll up tightly; secure with toothpicks. In a shallow bowl, combine the flour, Parmesan cheese, salt and pepper. Roll chicken in flour mixture; refrigerate for 1 hour.

In a skillet, brown roll-ups in oil on all sides; transfer to a slow cooker. Combine the soup and wine or broth; pour over chicken. Cover and cook on low for 4-5 hours or until a meat thermometer reads 170°. Remove roll-ups and stir sauce. Serve with rice. **Yield:** 6 servings.

Wild Rice Turkey Dinner

(Pictured below)

Cook Time: 7 to 8 Hours

Tabitha Dodge, Conover, Wisconsin

We live in the northwoods, and the wild rice, squash and cranberries I use for this impressive dish are locally grown.

3/4 cup uncooked wild rice
1 medium butternut squash, peeled, seeded and cut into 1-inch pieces
1 medium onion, cut into 1-inch pieces
2 turkey breast tenderloins (1/2 pound *each*)
3 cups chicken broth
1/2 teaspoon salt
1/2 teaspoon pepper
1/2 teaspoon dried thyme
1/2 cup dried cranberries

In a 5-qt. slow cooker, layer the rice, squash, onion and turkey. Add broth; sprinkle with salt, pepper and thyme. Cover and cook on low for 7-8 hours or until turkey juices run clear. Remove turkey; cut into slices. Stir cranberries into rice mixture; serve with a slotted spoon. **Yield:** 4 servings.

Wild Rice Turkey Dinner

Nostalgic Chicken and Dumplings

wine or additional broth over chicken mixture. Cover and cook on low for 4-1/2 to 5 hours or until chicken juices run clear and a meat thermometer reads 170°.

Remove chicken and keep warm. Discard cloves and bay leaf. Increase temperature to high. In a small bowl, combine cornstarch, water and browning sauce if desired until smooth. Stir into slow cooker.

In another bowl, combine biscuit mix, milk and parsley. Drop by tablespoonfuls onto simmering liquid. Cover and simmer for 20-25 minutes or until a toothpick inserted into dumplings comes out clean (do not lift cover while simmering). Serve dumplings and gravy over chicken. **Yield:** 6 servings.

Nostalgic Chicken And Dumplings

(Pictured above)

Cook Time: 5 to 5-1/2 Hours

Brenda Edwards, Hereford, Arizona

You'll enjoy old-fashioned goodness without all the fuss when you fix this supper in your slow cooker.

  6 **bone-in chicken breast halves (10 ounces each), skin removed**
  2 **whole cloves**
12 **frozen pearl or small whole onions, thawed**
  1 **bay leaf**
  1 **garlic clove, minced**
1/2 **teaspoon each salt, dried thyme and dried marjoram**
1/4 **teaspoon pepper**
1/2 **cup chicken broth**
1/2 **cup white wine or additional chicken broth**
  3 **tablespoons cornstarch**
1/4 **cup cold water**
1/2 **teaspoon browning sauce, optional**
  1 **cup biscuit/baking mix**
  6 **tablespoons milk**
  1 **tablespoon minced fresh parsley**

Place the chicken in a slow cooker. Insert cloves into an onion; add to slow cooker. Add bay leaf and remaining onions. Sprinkle chicken with garlic, salt, thyme, marjoram and pepper. Pour broth and

Lemony Turkey Breast

(Pictured below)

Cook Time: 5 to 7 Hours

Lynn Laux, Ballwin, Missouri

Lemon and a hint of garlic add a lovely touch to moist turkey breast slices. I usually serve the gravy over a combination of white and brown rice.

  1 **bone-in turkey breast (5 pounds), halved**
  1 **medium lemon, halved**
  1 **teaspoon lemon-pepper seasoning**
  1 **teaspoon garlic salt**
  4 **teaspoons cornstarch**
1/2 **cup chicken broth**

Remove skin from turkey. Pat turkey dry with paper towels; spray turkey with nonstick cooking spray. Place breast side up in a slow cooker. Squeeze half

Lemony Turkey Breast

of the lemon over turkey; sprinkle with lemon-pepper and garlic salt. Place lemon halves under turkey. Cover and cook on low for 5-7 hours or until meat is no longer pink and a meat thermometer reads 170°. Remove turkey and keep warm. Discard lemon.

For gravy, pour cooking liquid into a measuring cup; skim fat. In a saucepan, combine cornstarch and broth until smooth. Gradually stir in cooking liquid. Bring to a boil; cook and stir for 2 minutes or until thickened. Serve with turkey. **Yield:** 14 servings.

Red Pepper Chicken

Cook Time: 6 Hours

Piper Spiwak, Vienna, Virginia

Chicken breasts are treated to a bevy of black beans, red peppers and tomatoes in this southwestern supper. I chop an onion before putting everything in the slow cooker.

   4 boneless skinless chicken breast halves
   1 can (15 ounces) black beans, rinsed and
     drained
   1 jar (15 ounces) roasted red peppers,
     undrained
   1 can (14-1/2 ounces) Mexican stewed
     tomatoes, undrained
   1 large onion, chopped
 1/2 teaspoon salt
Pepper to taste
Hot cooked rice

Place the chicken in a slow cooker. In a bowl, combine the beans, red peppers, tomatoes, onion, salt and pepper. Pour over the chicken. Cover and cook on low for 6 hours or until chicken is no longer pink. Serve over rice. **Yield:** 4 servings.

Herbed Slow-Cooker Chicken

Cook Time: 4 to 5 Hours

Sundra Hauck, Bogalusa, Louisiana

These well-seasoned chicken breasts are easy and delicious. My daughter, who is busy with two young sons, shared this recipe with me several years ago.

   1 tablespoon olive oil
   1 teaspoon paprika
 1/2 teaspoon garlic powder
 1/2 teaspoon seasoned salt
 1/2 teaspoon dried thyme
 1/2 teaspoon dried basil
 1/2 teaspoon pepper
 1/2 teaspoon browning sauce, optional
   4 bone-in chicken breast halves
     (6 ounces *each*)
 1/2 cup chicken broth

Chicken Veggie Alfredo

In a small bowl, combine the first eight ingredients; rub over chicken. Place in a 5-qt. slow cooker; add chicken broth. Cover and cook on low for 4-5 hours or until a meat thermometer reads 170°. **Yield:** 4 servings.

Chicken Veggie Alfredo

(Pictured above)

Cook Time: 6 to 8 Hours

Jennifer Jordan, Hubbard, Ohio

My family loves this pasta-and-chicken dinner. If you like, add other veggies to suit your family's tastes.

   4 boneless skinless chicken breast halves
   1 tablespoon vegetable oil
   1 jar (16 ounces) Alfredo sauce
   1 can (15-1/4 ounces) whole kernel corn,
     drained
   1 cup frozen peas, thawed
   1 jar (4-1/2 ounces) sliced mushrooms,
     drained
 1/2 cup chopped onion
 1/2 cup water
 1/2 teaspoon garlic salt
 1/4 teaspoon pepper
Hot cooked linguine

In a large skillet, brown chicken in oil. Transfer to a slow cooker. In a bowl, combine the Alfredo sauce, corn, peas, mushrooms, onion, water, garlic salt and pepper. Pour over chicken. Cover and cook on low for 6-8 hours. Serve over linguine. **Yield:** 4 servings.

Pork, Lamb & Seafood

Slow-Cooked Cherry Pork Chops (p. 86)

Chapter 6

Slow-Cooked Lamb Chops

(Pictured below)

Cook Time: 5-1/2 to 7-1/2 Hours

Sandra McKenzie, Braham, Minnesota

This is my favorite recipe for lamb chops. It's great for people who are trying lamb for the first time, since the meat turns out extra tender and tasty. I decided to wrap the chops in bacon because that's how I've always prepared venison. I think it really enhances the flavor.

    4 **bacon strips**
    4 **lamb shoulder blade chops, trimmed**
2-1/4 **cups thinly sliced peeled potatoes**
    1 **cup thinly sliced carrots**
1/2 **teaspoon dried rosemary, crushed**
1/4 **teaspoon garlic powder**
1/4 **teaspoon salt**
1/4 **teaspoon pepper**
1/4 **cup chopped onion**
    2 **garlic cloves, minced**
    1 **can (10-3/4 ounces) condensed cream of mushroom soup, undiluted**
1/3 **cup milk**
    1 **jar (4-1/2 ounces) sliced mushrooms, drained**

Wrap bacon around lamb chops; secure with toothpicks. Place in a slow cooker. Cover and cook on high for 1-1/2 hours. Remove chops; discard toothpicks and bacon. Drain liquid from slow cooker. Add potatoes and carrots; top with lamb chops. Sprinkle with rosemary, garlic powder, salt, pepper, onion and garlic.

In a bowl, combine soup and milk; mix well. Add mushrooms. Pour over the chops. Cover and cook on low for 4-6 hours or until meat and vegetables are tender. **Yield:** 4 servings.

Slow-Cooked Lamb Chops

Cranberry Pork Tenderloin

Cranberry Pork Tenderloin

(Pictured above)

Cook Time: 5 to 6 Hours

Betty Helton, Melbourne, Florida

I use a can of cranberry sauce to dress up this no-fuss pork entree. Orange juice and cloves season it nicely.

    1 **pork tenderloin (1 pound)**
    1 **can (16 ounces) whole-berry cranberry sauce**
1/2 **cup orange juice**
1/4 **cup sugar**
    1 **tablespoon brown sugar**
    1 **teaspoon ground mustard**
1/4 **to 1/2 teaspoon ground cloves**
    2 **tablespoons cornstarch**
    3 **tablespoons cold water**

Place the pork tenderloin in a 3-qt. slow cooker. Combine the cranberry sauce, orange juice, sugars, mustard and cloves; pour over pork tenderloin. Cover and cook on low for 5-6 hours or until a meat thermometer reads 160°.

Remove the pork and keep warm. In a small saucepan, combine cornstarch and cold water until smooth; stir in cranberry mixture. Bring to a boil; cook and stir for 2 minutes or until thickened. Serve with pork. **Yield:** 4 servings.

Shredded Pork with Beans

Cook Time: 8 Hours

Sarah Johnston, Lincoln, Nebraska

A friend gave me this recipe, which my sons say is a keeper. For a change of pace, spoon the filling into taco shells.

    3 **pork tenderloins (about 1 pound *each*), cut into 3-inch pieces**
    2 **cans (15 ounces *each*) black beans, rinsed and drained**

1 jar (24 ounces) picante sauce
Hot cooked rice, optional

In a 5-qt. slow cooker, place the pork, beans and picante sauce. Cover and cook on low for 8 hours or until pork is tender. Shred pork; return to slow cooker. Serve with rice if desired. **Yield:** 10-12 servings.

Slow-Cooker Pork And Apple Curry

Cook Time: 5-1/2 to 6-1/2 Hours

Nancy Reck, Mill Valley, California

Here's a gentle curry dish that's sure to please American palates. Vary the garnish by adding peanuts or chutney.

    2 pounds boneless pork loin roast, cut
      into 1-inch cubes
    1 medium tart apple, peeled and chopped
    1 small onion, chopped
  1/2 cup orange juice
    1 tablespoon curry powder
    1 teaspoon chicken bouillon granules
    1 garlic clove, minced
  1/2 teaspoon salt
  1/2 teaspoon ground ginger
  1/4 teaspoon ground cinnamon
    2 tablespoons cornstarch
    2 tablespoons cold water
Hot cooked rice, optional
  1/4 cup raisins
  1/4 cup flaked coconut, toasted

In a 3-qt. slow cooker, combine the first 10 ingredients. Cover and cook on low for 5-6 hours or until meat is tender. Increase heat to high.

In a small bowl, combine cornstarch and water until smooth; stir into slow cooker. Cover and cook for 30 minutes or until thickened, stirring once. Serve over rice if desired. Sprinkle with raisins and coconut. **Yield:** 8 servings.

Brat Sauerkraut Supper

Cook Time: 4 to 5 Hours

Ann Christensen, Mesa, Arizona

This stick-to-your-ribs German dish satisfies even the biggest appetites. Serve it alongside rye bread for an entire meal.

    1 jar (32 ounces) sauerkraut, rinsed and
      drained
    2 medium red potatoes, peeled, halved and
      cut into thin slices
    1 medium tart apple, peeled and cut into
      thick slices
    1 small onion, chopped
  1/2 cup apple juice

  1/4 cup water
    2 tablespoons brown sugar
    1 teaspoon chicken bouillon granules
    1 teaspoon caraway seeds
    1 garlic clove, minced
    1 bay leaf
    1 pound fully cooked bratwurst links
    6 bacon strips, cooked and crumbled

In a 5-qt. slow cooker, combine the first 11 ingredients. Top with bratwurst. Cover and cook on high for 4-5 hours or until potatoes are tender. Discard bay leaf. Sprinkle with bacon. **Yield:** 6 servings.

Shrimp Marinara

(Pictured below)

Cook Time: 3-1/2 to 4-1/2 Hours

Sue Mackey, Galesburg, Illinois

I simmer this flavorful marinara sauce for most of the day. Then shortly before mealtime, I just add cooked shrimp.

    1 can (14-1/2 ounces) Italian diced tomatoes,
      undrained
    1 can (6 ounces) tomato paste
  1/2 to 1 cup water
    2 garlic cloves, minced
    2 tablespoons minced fresh parsley
    1 teaspoon salt, optional
    1 teaspoon dried oregano
  1/2 teaspoon dried basil
  1/4 teaspoon pepper
    1 pound fresh *or* frozen shrimp, cooked,
      peeled and deveined
    1 pound spaghetti, cooked and drained
Shredded Parmesan cheese, optional

In a slow cooker, combine the first nine ingredients. Cover and cook on low for 3-4 hours. Stir in shrimp. Cover and cook 20 minutes longer or just until shrimp are heated through. Serve over spaghetti. Garnish with cheese if desired. **Yield:** 6 servings.

Shrimp Marinara

Slow-Cooker Salmon Loaf

Slow-Cooker Salmon Loaf

(Pictured above)

Cook Time: 4 to 6 Hours

Kelly Ritter, Douglasville, Georgia

Taking care of my two small children, I'm always looking for quick, easy recipes that can be prepared ahead of time. I adapted this family-pleasing recipe from one I found in an old slow-cooker book of my grandma's.

> 2 eggs, lightly beaten
> 2 cups seasoned stuffing croutons
> 1 cup chicken broth
> 1 cup grated Parmesan cheese
> 1/4 teaspoon ground mustard
> 1 can (14-3/4 ounces) salmon, drained, bones and skin removed

In a bowl, combine the first five ingredients. Add salmon and mix well. Transfer to a slow cooker coated with nonstick cooking spray. Gently shape mixture into a loaf. Cover and cook on low for 4-6 hours or until a meat thermometer reads 160°. **Yield:** 6 servings.

Pennsylvania Pot Roast

Cook Time: 8 Hours

Donna Wilkinson, Clarksburg, Maryland

This heartwarming one-dish meal is adapted from a Pennsylvania Dutch recipe. I start the pot roast cooking before I leave for church and add the vegetables when I get home.

> 2-1/2 to 3 pounds boneless pork shoulder roast
> 1-1/2 cups beef broth
> 1/2 cup sliced green onions
> 1 teaspoon dried basil
> 1 teaspoon dried marjoram
> 1/2 teaspoon salt
> 1/2 teaspoon pepper
> 1 bay leaf
> 6 medium red potatoes, cut into 2-inch chunks
> 4 medium carrots, cut into 2-inch chunks
> 7 to 8 fresh mushrooms, quartered
> 1/4 cup all-purpose flour
> 1/2 cup cold water
> Browning sauce, optional

Cut roast in half. Place roast in a slow cooker; add broth, onions and seasonings. Cover and cook on high for 2 hours. Add potatoes, carrots and mushrooms. Cover and cook on low for 6 hours or until vegetables are tender.

Remove the meat and vegetables; keep warm. Discard bay leaf. In a saucepan, combine flour and cold water until smooth; stir in 1-1/2 cups cooking juices. Bring to a boil. Cook and stir for 2 minutes or until thickened. Add browning sauce if desired. Serve with roast and vegetables. **Yield:** 6 servings.

Citrus Pork Roast

Cook Time: 4 Hours

Tammy Logan, McComb, Ohio

The delicious hint of orange in the gravy served over these thick slices of pork roast makes them stand out from the crowd. Garlic, thyme and ginger enhance the great flavor.

> 1 boneless pork loin roast (about 3 pounds)
> 1/2 teaspoon garlic powder
> 1/2 teaspoon dried thyme
> 1/2 teaspoon ground ginger
> 1/4 teaspoon pepper
> 1 tablespoon vegetable oil
> 1 cup chicken broth
> 2 tablespoons sugar
> 2 tablespoons lemon juice
> 2 teaspoons soy sauce
> 1-1/2 teaspoons grated orange peel
> 3 tablespoons cornstarch
> 1/2 cup orange juice

Cut roast in half. In a small bowl, combine the garlic powder, thyme, ginger and pepper; rub over roast. In a large skillet over medium heat, brown roast on all sides in oil.

Place roast in a 5-qt. slow cooker. In a small bowl, combine the broth, sugar, lemon juice, soy sauce and orange peel; pour over roast. Cover and cook on low for 4 hours or until a meat thermometer reads 160°.

Remove roast and keep warm. In a saucepan, combine the cornstarch and orange juice until smooth; stir in cooking juices. Bring to a boil; cook and stir for 2 minutes or until thickened. Serve with the roast. **Yield:** 6-8 servings.

Pork Burritos

(Pictured below)

Cook Time: 8 to 10 Hours

Kelly Gengler, Theresa, Wisconsin

As a working mother, I depend on my slow cooker to help feed my family. We all love these tender burritos.

  1 boneless pork shoulder roast
    (3 to 4 pounds)
  1 can (14-1/2 ounces) diced tomatoes with
    mild green chilies, undrained
1/4 cup chili powder
  3 tablespoons minced garlic
  2 tablespoons lime juice
  2 tablespoons honey
  1 tablespoon chopped seeded jalapeno
    pepper
  1 teaspoon salt
 10 flour tortillas (8 inches), warmed
Sliced avocado and sour cream, optional

Cut roast in half; place in a 5-qt. slow cooker. In a blender, combine the tomatoes, chili powder, garlic, lime juice, honey, jalapeno and salt; cover and process until smooth. Pour over pork. Cover and cook on low for 8-10 hours or until meat is tender.

Shred pork with two forks. Using a slotted spoon, place about 1/2 cup pork mixture down the center of each tortilla; top with avocado and sour cream if desired. Fold sides and ends over filling and roll up. **Yield:** 10 burritos.

Editor's Note: When cutting or seeding hot peppers, use rubber or plastic gloves to protect your hands. Avoid touching your face.

Pork Burritos

Chops with Fruit Stuffing

Chops with Fruit Stuffing

(Pictured above)

Cook Time: 3 Hours

Suzanne Reyes, Tustin, California

The aroma that fills the house as this pork dish simmers is fabulous. All you need to complete the meal is a green vegetable and a loaf of bread.

  6 boneless pork loin chops (1/2 inch thick)
  1 tablespoon vegetable oil
  1 package (6 ounces) herb stuffing mix
  2 celery ribs, chopped
  1 medium tart apple, peeled and chopped
  1 cup dried cherries *or* cranberries
1/2 cup chopped onion
2/3 cup chicken broth
1/4 cup butter, melted

In a large skillet, brown pork chops in oil on both sides. In a large bowl, combine the remaining ingredients. Place half of the stuffing mixture in a 3-qt. slow cooker. Top with pork and remaining stuffing mixture. Cover and cook on low for 3 hours or until a meat thermometer reads 160°. **Yield:** 6 servings.

Try Buns Instead of Burritos

Need a sandwich recipe for a potluck, family gathering or other event? The flavorful shredded meat in Pork Burritos (recipe above left) is just as tasty served on buns. Eliminate the jalapenos if you want milder sandwiches.

Pork and Pinto Beans

(Pictured below)

Cook Time: 8 Hours

Darlene Brenden, Salem, Oregon

This is a great dish for company. I set out an array of toppings and let everyone fix their own taco salad.

- 1 **pound dried pinto beans**
- 1 **boneless pork loin roast (3 to 4 pounds), halved**
- 1 **can (14-1/2 ounces) stewed tomatoes**
- 5 **medium carrots, chopped**
- 4 **celery ribs, chopped**
- 1-1/2 **cups water**
- 2 **cans (4 ounces *each*) chopped green chilies**
- 2 **tablespoons chili powder**
- 4 **garlic cloves, minced**
- 2 **teaspoons ground cumin**
- 1 **teaspoon dried oregano**
- **Dash pepper**
- 2 **packages (10-1/2 ounces *each*) corn tortilla chips *or* 30 flour tortillas (9 inches)**
- **Chopped green onions, sliced ripe olives, chopped tomatoes, shredded cheddar cheese, sour cream *and/or* shredded lettuce**

Place beans in a saucepan; add water to cover by 2 in. Bring to a boil; boil for 2 minutes. Remove from the heat; cover and let stand for 1 hour.

Drain and rinse beans; discard liquid. Place roast in a 5-qt. slow cooker. In a bowl, combine the beans, tomatoes, carrots, celery, water, chilies, chili powder, garlic, cumin, oregano and pepper. Pour over roast.

Cover and cook on high for 3 hours. Reduce heat to low; cook 5 hours longer or until the beans are tender.

Remove meat; shred with two forks and return to slow cooker. With a slotted spoon, serve meat mixture over corn chips or in tortillas; serve with toppings of your choice. **Yield:** 10 servings.

Pizza Rigatoni

Cook Time: 4 Hours

Marilyn Cowan, North Manchester, Indiana

My slow cooker becomes a pizzeria when I make this zesty layered casserole loaded with cheese and sausage.

- 1-1/2 **pounds bulk Italian sausage**
- 3 **cups uncooked rigatoni *or* large tube pasta**
- 4 **cups (16 ounces) shredded part-skim mozzarella cheese**
- 1 **can (10-3/4 ounces) condensed cream of mushroom soup, undiluted**
- 1 **small onion, chopped**
- 2 **cans (one 15 ounces, one 8 ounces) pizza sauce**
- 1 **package (3-1/2 ounces) sliced pepperoni**
- 1 **can (6 ounces) pitted ripe olives, drained and halved**

In a skillet, cook sausage until no longer pink; drain. Cook pasta according to package directions; drain. In a 5-qt. slow cooker, layer half of the sausage, pasta, cheese, soup, onion, pizza sauce, pepperoni and olives. Repeat layers. Cover and cook on low for 4 hours. **Yield:** 6-8 servings.

Pork and Pinto Beans

Home-Style Ribs

Home-Style Ribs

(Pictured above)

Cook Time: 8 to 9 Hours

Roni Goodell, Spanish Fork, Utah

A dear friend of mine gave me the recipe for these effortless, tender ribs simmered in a pleasant barbecue sauce.

    4 to 5 pounds boneless pork spareribs, cut
      into pieces
    1 medium onion, thinly sliced
    1 cup ketchup
    1/2 to 1 cup water
    1/4 cup packed brown sugar
    1/4 cup cider vinegar
    2 tablespoons Worcestershire sauce
    2 teaspoons ground mustard
  1-1/2 teaspoons salt
    1 teaspoon paprika

Place half of the ribs in a slow cooker; top with half of the onion. Repeat layers. Combine the remaining ingredients; pour over all. Cover and cook on low for 8-9 hours or until ribs are tender. **Yield: 6-8 servings.**

Creamy Potatoes 'n' Kielbasa

Cook Time: 6 to 8 Hours

Beth Sine, Faulkner, Maryland

I need just five ingredients and my slow cooker to create this hearty meal-in-one. My whole family loves it.

    1 package (28 ounces) frozen O'Brien hash
      brown potatoes
    1 pound fully cooked kielbasa *or* Polish
      sausage, cut into 1/4-inch slices

    1 can (10-3/4 ounces) condensed cream of
      mushroom soup, undiluted
    1 cup (4 ounces) shredded cheddar cheese
  1/2 cup water

In a slow cooker, combine all ingredients. Cover and cook on low for 6-8 hours or until the potatoes are tender. **Yield:** 4-6 servings.

Spaghetti Pork Chops

(Pictured below)

Cook Time: 6 to 8 Hours

Ellen Gallavan, Midland, Michigan

These moist pork chops cook to perfection in a tangy tomato sauce. Served over pasta, this was one of my mother's most-loved recipes.

    3 cans (8 ounces *each*) tomato sauce
    1 can (10-3/4 ounces) condensed tomato
      soup, undiluted
    1 small onion, finely chopped
    1 bay leaf
    1 teaspoon celery seed
  1/2 teaspoon Italian seasoning
    6 bone-in pork chops (1 inch thick)
    2 tablespoons olive oil
  Hot cooked spaghetti

In a 5-qt. slow cooker, combine the tomato sauce, soup, onion, bay leaf, celery seed and Italian seasoning. In a large skillet, brown pork chops in oil. Add to the slow cooker. Cover and cook on low for 6-8 hours or until meat is tender. Discard bay leaf. Serve chops and sauce over spaghetti. **Yield:** 6 servings.

Spaghetti Pork Chops

Barbecued Pork Chop Supper

Barbecued Pork Chop Supper

(Pictured above)

Cook Time: 8 to 9 Hours

Jacqueline Jones, Round Lake Beach, Illinois

I start this dinner in the morning in my slow cooker and enjoy a tasty supper later without any last-minute work.

- 6 **small red potatoes, cut into quarters**
- 6 **medium carrots, cut into 1-inch pieces**
- 8 **bone-in pork loin *or* rib chops (1/2 inch thick)**
- 1 **teaspoon salt**
- 1/4 **teaspoon pepper**
- 1 **bottle (28 ounces) barbecue sauce**
- 1 **cup ketchup**
- 1 **cup cola**
- 2 **tablespoons Worcestershire sauce**

Place potatoes and carrots in a 5-qt. slow cooker. Top with pork chops. Sprinkle with salt and pepper. Combine the barbecue sauce, ketchup, cola and Worcestershire sauce; pour over chops. Cover and cook on low for 8-9 hours or until meat and vegetables are tender. **Yield:** 8 servings.

Italian Shrimp 'n' Pasta

(Pictured at right)

Cook Time: 7-1/2 to 8-1/2 Hours

Karen Scaglione, Nanuet, New York

This dish is always a hit! The shrimp, orzo, tomatoes and cayenne pepper remind me of a Creole favorite, but the Italian seasoning adds a different twist. The strips of chicken thighs stay nice and moist during the slow cooking.

- 1 **pound boneless skinless chicken thighs, cut into 2-inch x 1-inch strips**

- 2 **tablespoons vegetable oil**
- 1 **can (28 ounces) crushed tomatoes**
- 2 **celery ribs, chopped**
- 1 **medium green pepper, cut into 1-inch pieces**
- 1 **medium onion, coarsely chopped**
- 2 **garlic cloves, minced**
- 1 **tablespoon sugar**
- 1/2 **teaspoon salt**
- 1/2 **teaspoon Italian seasoning**
- 1/8 to 1/4 **teaspoon cayenne pepper**
- 1 **bay leaf**
- 1/2 **cup uncooked orzo pasta *or* other small pasta**
- 1 **pound cooked medium shrimp, peeled and deveined**

In a large skillet, brown chicken in oil; transfer to a 3-qt. slow cooker. Add the next 10 ingredients; mix well. Cover and cook on low for 7-8 hours or until chicken juices run clear. Discard bay leaf.

Stir in the pasta; cover and cook on high for 15 minutes or until pasta is tender. Stir in shrimp; cover and cook for 2 minutes or until the shrimp are heated through. **Yield:** 6-8 servings.

Cheesy Sausage Gravy

Cook Time: 7 to 8 Hours

P.J. Prusia, Raymore, Missouri

I appreciate the make-ahead convenience of this breakfast dish shared by a friend many years ago. When I serve this to overnight guests, they never fail to ask for the recipe.

- 1 **pound bulk pork sausage**
- 1/4 **cup butter**
- 1/4 **cup all-purpose flour**
- 1/4 **teaspoon pepper**
- 2-1/2 **cups milk**

Italian Shrimp 'n' Pasta

2 cans (10-3/4 ounces *each*) condensed
    cheddar cheese soup, undiluted
6 hard-cooked eggs, chopped
1 jar (4-1/2 ounces) sliced mushrooms,
    drained
Warm biscuits

In a large skillet, cook sausage over medium heat
until no longer pink; drain and remove sausage. In
the same skillet, melt butter. Stir in flour and pepper until smooth. Gradually whisk in milk. Bring to
a boil; cook and stir for 2 minutes or until thickened
and bubbly.

Stir in soup until blended. Stir in eggs, mushrooms and sausage. Transfer to a slow cooker. Cover and cook on low for 7-8 hours. Stir; serve over biscuits. **Yield:** 8 servings.

Slow-Cooked Ham 'n' Broccoli

Cook Time: 2 to 3 Hours

Jill Pennington, Jacksonville, Florida

*This sensational dish is so wonderful to come home to, especial-
ly on a cool fall or winter day. It's a delicious way to use up
leftover holiday ham, too.*

3 cups cubed fully cooked ham
1 package (10 ounces) frozen chopped
    broccoli, thawed
1 can (10-3/4 ounces) condensed cream of
    mushroom soup, undiluted
1 jar (8 ounces) process cheese sauce
1 can (8 ounces) sliced water chestnuts,
    drained
1-1/4 cups uncooked instant rice
1 cup milk
1 celery rib, chopped
1 medium onion, chopped
1/8 to 1/4 teaspoon pepper
1/2 teaspoon paprika

In a slow cooker, combine the first 10 ingredients; mix
well. Cover and cook on high for 2-3 hours or until
the rice is tender. Let stand for 10 minutes before
serving. Sprinkle with paprika. **Yield:** 6-8 servings.

Southwestern Pulled Pork

(Pictured above right)

Cook Time: 8 to 9 Hours

Jill Hartung, Colorado Springs, Colorado

*Bottled barbecue sauce, canned green chilies and a few other
kitchen staples make preparation of this seasoned pork fast and
easy. We like to wrap it in flour tortillas.*

2 cans (4 ounces *each*) chopped green chilies
1 can (8 ounces) tomato sauce

Southwestern Pulled Pork

1 cup barbecue sauce
1 large sweet onion, thinly sliced
1/4 cup chili powder
1 teaspoon ground cumin
1 teaspoon dried oregano
1 boneless pork loin roast (2 to 2-1/2 pounds)
Flour tortillas
**Toppings: sour cream, shredded lettuce and
    chopped tomatoes, optional**

In a 3-qt. slow cooker, combine the chilies, tomato
sauce, barbecue sauce, onion, chili powder, cumin
and oregano. Add pork. Cover and cook on low
for 8-9 hours or until meat is tender.

Remove pork. When cool enough to handle,
shred meat using two forks. Return to slow cooker
and heat through. Serve on tortillas; top with sour
cream, lettuce and tomatoes if desired. **Yield:** 6-8
servings.

Chinese Pork Ribs

Cook Time: 6 Hours

June Ross, Landing, New Jersey

*This is one of the only dishes that both of my young boys love—
they even come back for seconds. I also like that it requires just
a handful of ingredients.*

1/3 cup soy sauce
1/3 cup orange marmalade
3 tablespoons ketchup
2 garlic cloves, minced
3 to 4 pounds bone-in country-style pork ribs

In a bowl, combine the soy sauce, marmalade,
ketchup and garlic. Pour half into a slow cooker. Top
with ribs; drizzle with remaining sauce. Cover and
cook on low for 6 hours or until tender. Thicken
cooking juices if desired. **Yield:** 6-8 servings.

Burgundy Lamb Shanks

Cook Time: 8 Hours

Val Creutz, Southold, New York

For those who love fall-from-the-bone lamb, this recipe fills the bill. Burgundy wine adds a special touch to the sauce.

    4 lamb shanks (about 20 ounces *each*)
Salt and pepper to taste
    2 tablespoons dried parsley flakes
    2 teaspoons minced garlic
  1/2 teaspoon dried oregano
  1/2 teaspoon grated lemon peel
  1/2 cup chopped onion
    1 medium carrot, chopped
    1 teaspoon olive oil
    1 cup burgundy wine *or* beef broth
    1 teaspoon beef bouillon granules

Sprinkle lamb shanks with salt and pepper. Place in a 5-qt. slow cooker. Sprinkle with parsley, garlic, oregano and lemon peel.

In a small saucepan, saute the onion and carrot in oil for 3-4 minutes or until tender. Stir in wine or broth and bouillon. Bring to a boil, stirring occasionally. Pour over lamb. Cover and cook on low for 8 hours or until meat is tender.

Remove lamb and keep warm. Strain cooking juices and skim fat. In a small saucepan, bring juices to a boil; cook until liquid is reduced by half. Serve with lamb. **Yield:** 4 servings.

Slow-Cooked Ham

(Pictured below)

Cook Time: 8 to 10 Hours

Heather Spring, Sheppard Air Force Base, Texas

Entertaining doesn't get much easier than when you serve this tasty entree. Leftovers are delicious in casseroles.

Slow-Cooked Ham

  1/2 cup packed brown sugar
    1 teaspoon ground mustard
    1 teaspoon prepared horseradish
    4 tablespoons regular cola, *divided*
    1 boneless smoked ham (5 to 6 pounds), cut in half

In a bowl, combine the brown sugar, mustard, horseradish and 2 tablespoons cola; mix well. Rub over ham. Place in a 5-qt. slow cooker; pour remaining cola over ham. Cover and cook on low for 8-10 hours or until a meat thermometer reads 140°. **Yield:** 15-20 servings.

Sweet Sausage 'n' Beans

Cook Time: 4 Hours

Doris Heath, Franklin, North Carolina

This slow-cooker version of a traditional French dish is chock-full of beans, smoked sausage and vegetables.

  1/2 cup thinly sliced carrots
  1/2 cup chopped onion
    2 cups frozen lima beans, thawed
    2 cups frozen green beans, thawed
    1 pound fully cooked smoked sausage, cut into 1/4-inch slices
    1 can (16 ounces) baked beans
  1/2 cup ketchup
  1/3 cup packed brown sugar
    1 tablespoon cider vinegar
    1 teaspoon prepared mustard

In a slow cooker, layer carrots, onion, lima beans, green beans, sausage and baked beans. Combine ketchup, brown sugar, vinegar and mustard; pour over beans. Cover and cook on high for 4 hours or until vegetables are tender. Stir before serving. **Yield:** 4-6 servings.

Slow-Cooked Sweet 'n' Sour Pork

(Pictured above right)

Cook Time: 6-1/2 to 8-1/2 Hours

Martha Nickerson, Hancock, Maine

A coworker gave me this recipe more than 20 years ago, and my family still enjoys this satisfying entree today.

    2 tablespoons plus 1-1/2 teaspoons paprika
2-1/2 pounds boneless pork loin roast, cut into 1-inch strips
    1 tablespoon canola oil
    1 can (20 ounces) pineapple chunks
    1 medium onion, chopped
    1 medium green pepper, chopped

Slow-Cooked Sweet 'n' Sour Pork

1/4 cup cider vinegar
3 tablespoons brown sugar
3 tablespoons soy sauce
1 tablespoon Worcestershire sauce
1/2 teaspoon salt
2 tablespoons cornstarch
1/4 cup cold water
Hot cooked rice, optional

Place paprika in a large resealable plastic bag. Add pork, a few pieces at a time, and shake to coat. In a nonstick skillet, brown pork in oil in batches over medium-high heat. Transfer to a 3-qt. slow cooker.

Drain pineapple, reserving juice; refrigerate the pineapple. Add the pineapple juice, onion, green pepper, vinegar, brown sugar, soy sauce, Worcestershire sauce and salt to slow cooker; mix well. Cover and cook on low for 6-8 hours or until meat is tender. Combine cornstarch and water until smooth; stir into pork mixture. Add pineapple. Cover and cook 30 minutes longer or until sauce is thickened. Serve over rice if desired. **Yield:** 6 servings.

No-Fuss Pork and Sauerkraut

Cook Time: 4 to 5 Hours

Joan Pereira, Avon, Massachusetts

This home-style supper is just as easy as the name implies. I season the roast, then pop everything in the slow cooker.

1 boneless pork loin roast (4 to 5 pounds), quartered
1/3 cup Dijon mustard
1 teaspoon garlic powder
1 teaspoon rubbed sage
1 can (27 ounces) sauerkraut, drained
2 medium tart apples, sliced
1 cup apple juice

Rub roast with mustard; sprinkle with garlic powder and sage. Place sauerkraut and half of the apples

in a slow cooker. Top with roast. Pour apple juice around roast; top with remaining apples. Cover and cook on high for 4-5 hours or until a meat thermometer reads 160°. **Yield:** 12-16 servings.

Pork Chop Potato Dinner

(Pictured below)

Cook Time: 3 to 3-1/2 Hours

Dawn Huizinga, Owatonna, Minnesota

Juicy chops cook on a bed of creamy potatoes in this all-in-one meal. It's a snap to assemble, thanks to frozen hash browns, canned soup and french-fried onions.

6 bone-in pork chops (1/2 inch thick)
1 tablespoon vegetable oil
1 package (30 ounces) frozen shredded hash brown potatoes, thawed
1-1/2 cups (6 ounces) shredded cheddar cheese, *divided*
1 can (10-3/4 ounces) condensed cream of celery soup, undiluted
1/2 cup milk
1/2 cup sour cream
1/2 teaspoon seasoned salt
1/8 teaspoon pepper
1 can (2.8 ounces) french-fried onions, *divided*

In a large skillet, brown chops in oil on both sides; set aside and keep warm. In a bowl, combine the potatoes, 1 cup cheese, soup, milk, sour cream, seasoned salt and pepper. Stir in half of the onions.

Transfer to a greased 5-qt. slow cooker; top with pork chops. Cover and cook on high for 2-1/2 to 3 hours or until meat juices run clear. Sprinkle with remaining cheese and onions. Cover and cook 10 minutes longer or until cheese is melted. **Yield:** 6 servings.

Pork Chop Potato Dinner

Slow-Cooked Cherry Pork Chops

2 celery ribs, cut in half
2 teaspoons minced garlic, *divided*
1 teaspoon whole peppercorns
1/2 cup barbecue sauce
1/4 cup plum sauce
Dash hot pepper sauce

Place the ribs in a 5-qt. slow cooker. Add the water, onion, celery, 1 teaspoon garlic and peppercorns. Cover and cook on low for 6 hours or until meat is tender.

In a small saucepan, combine the barbecue sauce, plum sauce, hot pepper sauce and remaining garlic. Cook and stir over medium heat for 5 minutes or until heated through. Remove ribs. Discard cooking juices and vegetables.

Coat grill rack with nonstick cooking spray before starting the grill. Brush ribs with sauce. Grill, uncovered, over medium-low heat for 8-10 minutes or until browned, turning occasionally and brushing with remaining sauce. **Yield:** 4 servings.

Slow-Cooked Cherry Pork Chops

(Pictured above and on page 74)

Cook Time: 3 to 4 Hours

Mildred Sherrer, Bay City, Texas

I mixed and matched several recipes to come up with this one. It's so simple to prepare in the slow cooker.

    6 bone-in pork loin chops (3/4 inch thick)
1/8 teaspoon salt
Dash pepper
    1 cup canned cherry pie filling
    2 teaspoons lemon juice
1/2 teaspoon chicken bouillon granules
1/8 teaspoon ground mace

In a skillet coated with nonstick cooking spray, brown the pork chops over medium heat on both sides. Season with salt and pepper.

In a slow cooker, combine pie filling, lemon juice, bouillon and mace. Add pork chops. Cover and cook on low for 3-4 hours or until meat is no longer pink. **Yield:** 6 servings.

Baby Back Ribs

(Pictured at right)

Cook Time: 6 Hours

After these saucy ribs from our Test Kitchen staff are done in the slow cooker, they go on the grill for unbeatable flavor.

2-1/2 pounds pork baby back ribs, cut into eight pieces
    5 cups water
    1 medium onion, sliced

Pork 'n' Pepper Tortillas

Cook Time: 8 to 9 Hours

Rita Hahnbaum, Muscatine, Iowa

I season this pork roast and cook it slowly until tender. Then I shred the flavorful meat and wrap it along with colorful peppers in warm tortillas.

    1 bone-in pork shoulder roast (3 to 4 pounds)
    1 cup boiling water
    2 teaspoons beef bouillon granules
    3 garlic cloves, minced
    1 tablespoon dried basil
    1 tablespoon dried oregano
    1 teaspoon ground cumin

Baby Back Ribs

1 teaspoon pepper
1 teaspoon dried tarragon
1 teaspoon white pepper
2 medium onions, sliced
1 *each* large green, sweet red and yellow
 pepper, sliced
1 tablespoon butter
12 to 14 flour tortillas (7 inches), warmed
Shredded lettuce, chopped ripe olives, sliced
 jalapeno peppers and sour cream, optional

Cut roast into quarters; place in a 5-qt. slow cooker. Combine water, bouillon, garlic and seasonings; pour over roast. Top with onions. Cover and cook on high for 1 hour. Reduce heat to low. Cook for 7-8 hours or until pork is very tender.

When cool enough to handle, remove meat from bone. Shred meat and return to slow cooker; heat through. Meanwhile, in a skillet, saute peppers in butter until tender. Using a slotted spoon, place about 1/2 cup pork and onion mixture down the center of each tortilla; top with peppers. Add lettuce, olives, jalapenos and sour cream if desired. Fold sides of tortilla over filling; serve immediately. **Yield:** 12-14 servings.

Ham Tetrazzini

Cook Time: 4 Hours

Susan Blair, Sterling, Michigan

I modified a recipe that came with my slow cooker to create this satisfying main dish. I've served it at countless parties, family dinners and potlucks.

1 can (10-3/4 ounces) condensed cream of
 mushroom soup, undiluted
1 cup sliced fresh mushrooms
1 cup cubed fully cooked ham
1/2 cup evaporated milk
2 tablespoons white wine *or* water
1 teaspoon prepared horseradish
1 package (7 ounces) spaghetti
1/2 cup shredded Parmesan cheese

In a slow cooker, combine the soup, mushrooms, ham, milk, wine or water and horseradish. Cover and cook on low for 4 hours. Cook spaghetti according to package directions; drain. Add the spaghetti and cheese to slow cooker; toss to coat. **Yield:** 6 servings.

Garlic-Apple Pork Roast

(Pictured above right)

Cook Time: 8 to 8-1/2 Hours

Jennifer Loos, Washington Boro, Pennsylvania

This is the meal I have become famous for, and it's so simple. The garlic and apple flavors really complement the pork.

Garlic-Apple Pork Roast

1 boneless whole pork loin roast (3-1/2 to 4
 pounds)
1 jar (12 ounces) apple jelly
1/2 cup water
2-1/2 teaspoons minced garlic
1 tablespoon dried parsley flakes
1 to 1-1/2 teaspoons seasoned salt
1 to 1-1/2 teaspoons pepper

Cut the roast in half; place in a 5-qt. slow cooker. In a bowl, combine the jelly, water and garlic; pour over roast. Sprinkle with parsley, salt and pepper. Cover and cook on low for 8 to 8-1/2 hours or until a meat thermometer reads 160° and meat is tender.

Let stand for 5 minutes before slicing. Serve with cooking juices if desired. **Yield:** 12 servings.

Crock O' Brats

Cook Time: 4 to 6 Hours

Maryellen Boettcher, Fairchild, Wisconsin

This all-in-one meal offers a hearty combination—slices of bratwurst take center stage alongside potatoes, sauerkraut, apple and onion.

5 bratwurst links (about 1-1/4 pounds), cut
 into 1-inch pieces
5 medium potatoes, peeled and cubed
1 can (27 ounces) sauerkraut, rinsed and well
 drained
1 medium tart apple, chopped
1 small onion, chopped
1/4 cup packed brown sugar
1/2 teaspoon salt

In a large skillet, brown bratwurst on all sides. In a 5-qt. slow cooker, combine the remaining ingredients. Stir in bratwurst and pan drippings. Cover and cook on high for 4-6 hours or until potatoes and apple are tender. **Yield:** 6 servings.

Cider Pork Roast

Potato Sausage Supper

Cook Time: 6 Hours

Patricia Ginn, Delphi, Indiana

I've taken this comforting, layered casserole to family reunions and always return with an empty slow cooker.

- 4 medium potatoes, peeled and sliced
- 1 pound fully cooked kielbasa *or* Polish sausage, cut into 1/2-inch slices
- 2 medium onions, sliced and separated into rings
- 1 can (10-3/4 ounces) condensed cheddar cheese soup, undiluted
- 1 can (10-3/4 ounces) condensed cream of celery soup, undiluted
- 1 package (10 ounces) frozen peas, thawed

In a greased 5-qt. slow cooker, layer a third of the potatoes, sausage, onions and cheese soup. Repeat layers twice.

Pour cream of celery soup over the top. Cover and cook on low for 5-1/2 hours or until the potatoes are tender. Add the peas and cook 30 minutes longer. **Yield:** 6-8 servings.

Cider Pork Roast

(Pictured above)

Cook Time: 5 to 6 Hours

Terry Danner, Rochelle, Illinois

Apple cider, dried cherries and fresh rosemary put the pizzazz in this family-pleasing pork roast.

- 1 boneless pork loin roast (2 pounds)
- 3/4 teaspoon salt
- 1/4 teaspoon pepper
- 2 cups apple cider *or* unsweetened apple juice, *divided*
- 3 sprigs fresh rosemary
- 1/2 cup dried cherries
- 5 teaspoons cornstarch

Sprinkle pork with salt and pepper. In a nonstick skillet coated with nonstick cooking spray, brown pork for about 4 minutes on each side. Pour 1 cup apple cider in a 3-qt. slow cooker. Place two sprigs rosemary in slow cooker; top with meat and remaining rosemary. Place cherries around roast. Cover and cook on low for 5-6 hours or until a meat thermometer reads 160°.

Remove meat; keep warm. Strain cooking liquid; reserve liquid and transfer to a small saucepan. Stir in 3/4 cup cider; bring to a boil. Combine cornstarch and remaining cider until smooth. Gradually whisk into cider mixture. Bring to a boil; cook and stir for 1-2 minutes or until thickened. Serve with meat. **Yield:** 6 servings.

Sweet 'n' Sour Sausage

(Pictured below and on back cover)

Cook Time: 4 to 5 Hours

Barbara Schutz, Pandora, Ohio

Carrots, green pepper and pineapple lend gorgeous color to this sausage supper served over rice.

- 1 pound fully cooked kielbasa *or* Polish sausage, sliced
- 1 can (20 ounces) unsweetened pineapple chunks, undrained
- 1-1/2 cups baby carrots, quartered lengthwise

Sweet 'n' Sour Sausage

1 large green pepper, cut into 1-inch pieces
1 medium onion, cut into chunks
1/3 cup packed brown sugar
1 tablespoon soy sauce
1/2 teaspoon chicken bouillon granules
1/4 teaspoon garlic powder
1/4 teaspoon ground ginger
2 tablespoons cornstarch
1/4 cup cold water
Hot cooked rice *or* chow mein noodles

In a slow cooker, combine the first 10 ingredients. Cover and cook on low for 4-5 hours; drain. In a small saucepan, combine the cornstarch and water until smooth. Bring to a boil; cook and stir for 1 minute or until thickened. Stir into the sausage mixture. Serve over rice. **Yield:** 6 servings.

Chili Casserole

Cook Time: 7 Hours

Marietta Slater, Augusta, Kansas

Even people who try to bypass casseroles can't stay away from this zesty meat-and-rice hot dish. The combination of seasonings makes it irresistible.

1 pound bulk pork sausage
2 cups water
1 can (15-1/2 ounces) chili beans, undrained
1 can (14-1/2 ounces) diced tomatoes, undrained
3/4 cup uncooked long grain rice
1/4 cup chopped onion
1 tablespoon chili powder
1 teaspoon Worcestershire sauce
1 teaspoon prepared mustard
3/4 teaspoon salt
1/8 teaspoon garlic powder
1 cup (4 ounces) shredded cheddar cheese

In a skillet, cook sausage until no longer pink; drain. Transfer to a slow cooker. Add the next 10 ingredients; stir well. Cover and cook on low for 7 hours or until rice is tender. Stir in cheese during the last 10 minutes of cooking time. **Yield:** 6 servings.

German-Style Short Ribs

(Pictured above right)

Cook Time: 8 to 10 Hours

Bregitte Rugman, Shanty Bay, Ontario

Our whole family is excited when I plug in the slow cooker to make these fall-off-the-bone-tender ribs.

3/4 cup dry red wine *or* beef broth
1/2 cup mango chutney
3 tablespoons quick-cooking tapioca

German-Style Short Ribs

1/4 cup water
3 tablespoons brown sugar
3 tablespoons cider vinegar
1 tablespoon Worcestershire sauce
1/2 teaspoon salt
1/2 teaspoon ground mustard
1/2 teaspoon chili powder
1/2 teaspoon pepper
4 pounds bone-in beef short ribs
2 medium onions, sliced
Hot cooked egg noodles

In a 5-qt. slow cooker, combine the first 11 ingredients. Add ribs and turn to coat. Top with onions. Cover and cook on low for 8-10 hours or until meat is tender. Remove ribs from slow cooker. Skim fat from cooking juices; serve over ribs and noodles. **Yield:** 8 servings.

Cabbage Kielbasa Supper

Cook Time: 8 to 9 Hours

Margery Bryan, Royal City, Washington

If you're a fan of German food, you'll enjoy this traditional combination of sausage, cabbage and potatoes. All you need is a bowl of fruit, and dinner's ready.

8 cups coarsely shredded cabbage
3 medium potatoes, cut into 1/2-inch cubes
1 medium onion, chopped
1-3/4 teaspoons salt
1/4 teaspoon pepper
1 can (14-1/2 ounces) chicken broth
2 pounds fully cooked kielbasa *or* Polish sausage, cut into serving-size pieces

In a 5-qt. slow cooker, combine the cabbage, potatoes, onion, salt and pepper. Pour broth over all. Place sausage on top (slow cooker will be full, but cabbage will cook down). Cover and cook on low for 8-9 hours or until vegetables are tender and sausage is heated through. **Yield:** 6-8 servings.

Meatless & Side Dishes

Roasted Red Pepper Sauce (p. 94)

Chapter 7

Sausage Spanish Rice

Sausage Spanish Rice

(Pictured above)

Cook Time: 5 to 6 Hours

Michelle McKay, Garden City, Michigan

My husband and I both work the midnight shift, so I'm always on the lookout for slow-cooker recipes. This one is good either as a side dish or a main course.

>   1 pound fully cooked kielbasa *or* Polish
>   sausage, cut into 1/4-inch slices
>   2 cans (14-1/2 ounces *each*) diced tomatoes,
>   undrained
>   2 cups water
> 1-1/2 cups uncooked converted rice
>   1 cup salsa
>   1 medium onion
>   1/2 cup chopped green pepper
>   1/2 cup chopped sweet red pepper
>   1 can (4 ounces) chopped green chilies
>   1 envelope taco seasoning

In a slow cooker, combine all ingredients; stir to blend. Cover and cook on low for 5-6 hours or until rice is tender. **Yield:** 9 servings.

   Editor's Note: This recipe was tested with Uncle Ben's converted rice.

Marmalade-Glazed Carrots

(Pictured at right)

Cook Time: 5-1/2 to 6-1/2 Hours

Barb Rudyk, Vermilion, Alberta

This delicious side dish is ideal for just about any occasion, from a weeknight supper to a special dinner. Cinnamon and nutmeg

nicely season baby carrots simmered with orange marmalade and brown sugar.

>   1 package (2 pounds) fresh baby carrots
>   1/2 cup orange marmalade
>   3 tablespoons cold water, *divided*
>   2 tablespoons brown sugar
>   1 tablespoon butter, melted
>   1/2 teaspoon ground cinnamon
>   1/4 teaspoon salt
>   1/4 teaspoon ground nutmeg
>   1/8 teaspoon pepper
>   1 tablespoon cornstarch

In a 3-qt. slow cooker, combine the carrots, marmalade, 1 tablespoon water, brown sugar, butter and seasonings. Cover and cook on low for 5-6 hours or until carrots are tender.
   Combine cornstarch and remaining water until smooth; stir into carrot mixture. Cover and cook on high for 30 minutes or until thickened. Serve with a slotted spoon. **Yield:** 6 servings.

Squash Stuffing Casserole

Cook Time: 4 to 5 Hours

Pamela Thorson, Hot Springs, Arkansas

My friends just rave about this creamy casserole. The vegetables are jazzed up with canned soup and stuffing mix.

>   1/4 cup all-purpose flour
>   1 can (10-3/4 ounces) condensed cream of
>   chicken soup, undiluted
>   1 cup (8 ounces) sour cream
>   2 medium yellow summer squash, cut into
>   1/2-inch slices

Marmalade-Glazed Carrots

2 medium zucchini, cut into 1/2-inch slices
1 small onion, chopped
1 cup shredded carrots
1 package (8 ounces) stuffing mix
1/2 cup butter, melted

In a bowl, combine the flour, soup and sour cream until blended. Add the vegetables and gently stir to coat. Combine the stuffing mix and butter; sprinkle half into a 5-qt. slow cooker. Top with vegetable mixture and remaining stuffing mixture. Cover and cook on low for 4-5 hours or until vegetables are tender. **Yield:** 8 servings.

Hearty Pork 'n' Beans

Cook Time: 4 to 5 Hours

Janice Toms, Saline, Louisiana

These slightly sweet beans taste great as a side dish and also as a main dish with French bread or corn bread.

1 pound ground beef
1 medium green pepper, chopped
1 small onion, chopped
1 package (16 ounces) smoked sausage, halved lengthwise and thinly sliced
1 can (16 ounces) pork and beans, undrained
1 can (15-1/4 ounces) lima beans, rinsed and drained
1 can (15 ounces) pinto beans, rinsed and drained
1 cup ketchup
1/2 cup packed brown sugar
1 teaspoon salt
1/2 teaspoon garlic powder
1/4 teaspoon pepper

In a skillet, cook beef, green pepper and onion over medium heat until meat is no longer pink; drain. In a slow cooker, combine the remaining ingredients. Stir in beef mixture. Cover and cook on high for 4-5 hours or until heated through. **Yield:** 8 main-dish servings or 12 side-dish servings.

Scalloped Taters

(Pictured above right)

Cook Time: 4-1/2 to 5 Hours

Lucinda Walker, Somerset, Pennsylvania

This creamy and comforting dish is a snap to assemble with frozen hash browns. It's a good way to make potatoes when your oven is busy with other dishes.

1 package (2 pounds) frozen cubed hash brown potatoes
1 can (10-3/4 ounces) condensed cream of chicken soup, undiluted

Scalloped Taters

1-1/2 cups milk
1 cup (4 ounces) shredded cheddar cheese
1/2 cup plus 1 tablespoon butter, melted, *divided*
1/4 cup dried minced onion
1/2 teaspoon salt
1/8 teaspoon pepper
3/4 cup crushed cornflakes

In a large bowl, combine hash browns, soup, milk, cheese, 1/2 cup butter, onion, salt and pepper. Pour into a greased 5-qt. slow cooker. Cover and cook on low for 4-1/2 to 5 hours or until potatoes are tender.

Just before serving, combine the cornflake crumbs and remaining butter in a pie plate. Bake at 350° for 4-6 minutes or until golden brown. Stir the potatoes; sprinkle with crumb topping. **Yield:** 12 servings.

Brunch Is a Breeze

As a side dish for dinner, tasty Scalloped Taters (recipe at left) is a sure winner. But you'll want to keep this appealing accompaniment in mind for meals in the morning, too.

That's because these easy-to-fix potatoes are convenient to have in your slow cooker while you're busy preparing an egg bake, pancakes, sausages or other brunch dishes on the stovetop or in the oven.

Just assemble the cheesy spuds first thing in the morning, and by the time you're ready to serve brunch, you'll have home-style hash brown potatoes everyone will love.

Roasted Red Pepper Sauce

(Pictured below and on page 90)

Cook Time: 4 Hours

Genie Tosh, Lumberton, New Jersey

I often use Greek olives with the artichoke hearts to add zing to this sauce. Roast the peppers yourself if you have time.

- 4 **pounds plum tomatoes (about 17), coarsely chopped**
- 1 **large sweet onion, chopped**
- 1 **can (29 ounces) tomato puree**
- 3 **jars (7 ounces *each*) roasted sweet red peppers, drained and chopped**
- 2 **jars (6-1/2 ounces *each*) marinated artichoke hearts, drained and chopped**
- 1/2 **pound fresh mushrooms, quartered**
- 2 **cans (2-1/4 ounces *each*) sliced ripe olives, drained**
- 1/4 **cup sugar**
- 1/4 **cup balsamic vinegar**
- 1/4 **cup olive oil**
- 3 **garlic cloves, minced**
- 1 **tablespoon dried basil**
- 1 **tablespoon dried oregano**
- 1 **teaspoon salt**

Hot cooked pasta

In a 5-qt. slow cooker, combine the first 14 ingredients. Cover and cook on high for 4 hours or until the flavors are blended. Serve over the pasta. **Yield:** about 15 cups.

Roasted Red Pepper Sauce

Corn Spoon Bread

Cook Time: 3 to 4 Hours

Tamara Ellefson, Frederic, Wisconsin

I prepare this versatile side dish with all of my holiday meals. It's moister than corn pudding made in the oven, and the cream cheese is a delicious addition.

- 1 **package (8 ounces) cream cheese, softened**
- 1/3 **cup sugar**
- 1 **cup milk**
- 1/2 **cup egg substitute**
- 2 **tablespoons butter, melted**
- 1 **teaspoon salt**
- 1/4 **teaspoon ground nutmeg**

Dash pepper

- 2-1/3 **cups frozen corn, thawed**
- 1 **can (14-3/4 ounces) cream-style corn**
- 1 **package (8-1/2 ounces) corn bread/muffin mix**

In a large mixing bowl, beat cream cheese and sugar until smooth. Gradually beat in milk. Beat in the egg substitute, butter, salt, nutmeg and pepper until blended. Stir in corn and cream-style corn.

Stir in bread mix just until moistened. Pour into a greased 3-qt. slow cooker. Cover and cook on high for 3-4 hours or until center is almost set. **Yield:** 8 servings.

Vegetable-Stuffed Peppers

Cook Time: 8-1/4 Hours

Sandra Allen, Austin, Texas

This recipe came with my slow cooker. The stuffed green peppers are filled with a flavorful combination of cooked rice, kidney beans, corn and onion. I like to fix meatless main dishes for a change of pace, and this tasty entree has become a monthly mainstay for my family.

- 2 **cans (14-1/2 ounces *each*) diced tomatoes, undrained**
- 1 **can (16 ounces) kidney beans, rinsed and drained**
- 1-1/2 **cups cooked rice**
- 2 **cups (8 ounces) shredded cheddar cheese, *divided***
- 1 **package (10 ounces) frozen corn, thawed**
- 1/4 **cup chopped onion**
- 1 **teaspoon Worcestershire sauce**
- 3/4 **teaspoon chili powder**
- 1/2 **teaspoon pepper**
- 1/4 **teaspoon salt**
- 6 **medium green peppers**

In a large bowl, combine the tomatoes, beans, rice, 1-1/2 cups cheese, corn, onion, Worcestershire

Egg and Broccoli Casserole

sauce, chili powder, pepper and salt; mix well. Remove and discard tops and seeds of green peppers. Fill each pepper with about 1 cup of the vegetable mixture. Place in a 5-qt. slow cooker. Cover and cook on low for 8 hours.

Sprinkle with remaining cheese. Cover and cook 15 minutes longer or until peppers are tender and cheese is melted. **Yield:** 6 servings.

Egg and Broccoli Casserole

(Pictured above)

Cook Time: 3-1/2 to 4 Hours

Janet Sliter, Kennewick, Washington

For years, I've prepared these filling eggs in my slow cooker. It's an unusual recipe for this appliance, but I get raves whenever I serve it. I think this cheesy dish is especially nice for brunch on Sundays, on holidays or when we have guests. The casserole doesn't take long to cook, so I can assemble it early in the morning and have it ready for breakfast.

    1 carton (24 ounces) small-curd cottage
      cheese
    1 package (10 ounces) frozen chopped
      broccoli, thawed and drained
    2 cups (8 ounces) shredded cheddar cheese
    6 eggs, beaten
  1/3 cup all-purpose flour
  1/4 cup butter, melted
    3 tablespoons finely chopped onion
  1/2 teaspoon salt
Additional shredded cheddar cheese, optional

In a large bowl, combine the first eight ingredients. Pour into a greased slow cooker. Cover and

cook on high for 1 hour. Stir. Reduce heat to low; cover and cook 2-1/2 to 3 hours longer or until a thermometer placed in the center reads 160° and the eggs are set. Sprinkle with cheese if desired. **Yield:** 6 servings.

Slow-Cooked Fruit Salad

(Pictured below)

Cook Time: 2 Hours

Debbie Kimbrough, Lexington, Mississippi

This down-home delight is so convenient when your oven and stovetop are occupied with other items.

  3/4 cup sugar
  1/2 cup butter, melted
  1/4 teaspoon ground cinnamon
  1/4 teaspoon ground nutmeg
  1/8 teaspoon salt
    2 cans (15-1/4 ounces *each*) sliced peaches,
      drained
    2 cans (15-1/4 ounces *each*) sliced pears,
      undrained
    1 jar (23 ounces) chunky applesauce
  1/2 cup dried apricots, chopped
  1/4 cup dried cranberries

In a 3-qt. slow cooker, combine the sugar, butter, cinnamon, nutmeg and salt. Stir in the remaining ingredients. Cover and cook on high for 2 hours or until heated through. **Yield:** 10 servings.

Slow-Cooked Fruit Salad

Saucy Red Potatoes

(Pictured below)

Cook Time: 5 to 6 Hours

Elaine Ryan, Holley, New York

These cubed spuds are cooked in a cheesy coating until tender. Be sure to stir the can't-miss dinner accompaniment before serving to help the sauce thicken.

> 7 cups cubed uncooked red potatoes
> 1 cup (8 ounces) small-curd cottage cheese
> 1/2 cup sour cream
> 1/2 cup cubed process cheese (Velveeta)
> 1 tablespoon dried minced onion
> 2 garlic cloves, minced
> 1/2 teaspoon salt
> **Paprika and minced chives, optional**

Place the potatoes in a slow cooker. In a blender or food processor, puree cottage cheese and sour cream until smooth. Transfer to a bowl; stir in the process cheese, onion, garlic and salt. Pour over potatoes and mix well.

Cover and cook on low for 5-6 hours or until the potatoes are tender. Stir well before serving. Garnish potatoes with paprika and minced chives if desired. **Yield:** 8 servings.

Mushroom Potatoes

Cook Time: 6 to 8 Hours

Linda Bernard, Golden Meadow, Louisiana

I jazz up sliced potatoes with mushrooms, onions, canned soup and cheese to create this versatile favorite.

> 7 medium potatoes, peeled and thinly sliced
> 1 medium onion, sliced
> 4 garlic cloves, minced
> 2 green onions, chopped
> 1 can (8 ounces) mushroom stems and pieces, drained
> 1/4 cup all-purpose flour
> 2 teaspoons salt
> 1/2 teaspoon pepper
> 1/4 cup butter, cubed
> 1 can (10-3/4 ounces) condensed cream of mushroom soup, undiluted
> 1 cup (4 ounces) shredded Colby-Monterey Jack cheese

In a slow cooker, layer half of the potatoes, onion, garlic, green onions, mushrooms, flour, salt, pepper and butter. Repeat layers. Pour soup over the top. Cover and cook on low for 6-8 hours or until potatoes are tender; sprinkle with cheese during the last 30 minutes of cooking time. **Yield:** 8-10 servings.

Saucy Red Potatoes

Meatless & Side Dishes

Slow-Cooked Beans

Slow-Cooked Beans

(Pictured above)

Cook Time: 2 Hours

Joy Beck, Cincinnati, Ohio

This flavorful bean dish adds nice variety to any buffet because it's a bit different than traditional baked beans.

- 4 cans (15-1/2 ounces *each*) great northern beans, rinsed and drained
- 4 cans (15 ounces *each*) black beans, rinsed and drained
- 2 cans (15 ounces *each*) butter beans, rinsed and drained
- 2-1/4 cups barbecue sauce
- 2-1/4 cups salsa
- 3/4 cup packed brown sugar
- 1/2 to 1 teaspoon hot pepper sauce

In a 5-qt. slow cooker, gently combine all ingredients. Cover and cook on low for 2 hours or until heated through. **Yield:** 16 servings.

Barbecued Beans

Cook Time: 10 to 12 Hours

Diane Hixon, Niceville, Florida

Most members of my family would agree that no picnic is complete until these delicious beans have made their appearance. They're easy to transport in the slow cooker.

- 1 pound dry navy beans
- 1 pound sliced bacon, cooked and crumbled
- 1 bottle (32 ounces) tomato juice
- 1 can (8 ounces) tomato sauce
- 2 cups chopped onion
- 2/3 cup packed brown sugar
- 1 tablespoon soy sauce
- 2 teaspoons garlic salt

- 1 teaspoon Worcestershire sauce
- 1 teaspoon ground mustard

Place beans in a 3-qt. saucepan; cover with water. Bring to a boil; boil for 2 minutes. Remove from the heat; let stand for 1 hour.

Drain beans and discard liquid. In a 5-qt. slow cooker, combine remaining ingredients; mix well. Add the beans. Cover and cook on high for 2 hours. Reduce heat to low and cook 8-10 hours longer or until beans are tender. **Yield:** 12-15 servings.

Sausage Dressing

(Pictured below)

Cook Time: 4 to 5 Hours

Mary Kendall, Appleton, Wisconsin

I relied on this slow cooker recipe one Thanksgiving when there was no room in my oven to bake stuffing. The results were fantastic—very moist and flavorful.

- 1 pound bulk pork sausage
- 1 large onion, chopped
- 2 celery ribs, chopped
- 1 package (14 ounces) seasoned stuffing croutons
- 1 can (14-1/2 ounces) chicken broth
- 1 large tart apple, chopped
- 1 cup chopped walnuts *or* pecans
- 1/2 cup egg substitute
- 1/4 cup butter, melted
- 1-1/2 teaspoons rubbed sage
- 1/2 teaspoon pepper

In a large skillet, cook the sausage, onion and celery over medium heat until meat is no longer pink; drain. Transfer to a greased 5-qt. slow cooker. Stir in remaining ingredients. Cover and cook on low for 4-5 hours or until heated through. **Yield:** 12 servings.

Sausage Dressing

Au Gratin Garlic Potatoes

Au Gratin Garlic Potatoes

(Pictured above)

Cook Time: 6 to 7 Hours

Tonya Vowels, Vine Grove, Kentucky

Cream cheese and cheese soup turn ordinary potatoes into this rich specialty that's perfect with almost any meal.

- 1/2 cup milk
- 1 can (10-3/4 ounces) condensed cheddar cheese soup, undiluted
- 1 package (8 ounces) cream cheese, cubed
- 1 garlic clove, minced
- 1/4 teaspoon ground nutmeg
- 1/8 teaspoon pepper
- 2 pounds potatoes, peeled and sliced
- 1 small onion, chopped
- Paprika, optional

In a saucepan, heat milk over medium heat until bubbles form around side of saucepan. Remove from the heat. Add the soup, cream cheese, garlic, nutmeg and pepper; stir until smooth.

Place the potatoes and onion in a 3-qt. slow cooker. Pour the milk mixture over the potato mixture; mix well. Cover and cook on low for 6-7 hours or until potatoes are tender. Sprinkle with paprika if desired. **Yield:** 6-8 servings.

Pineapple Baked Beans

Cook Time: 4 to 8 Hours

Gladys De Boer, Castleford, Idaho

Sweet bits of pineapple dress up these tangy beans, which get even more flavor from ground beef, barbecue sauce, soy sauce, vegetables and garlic. Brown the beef while you open the cans and chop the veggies, and it won't take long to get this ready for the slow cooker.

- 1 pound ground beef
- 1 can (28 ounces) baked beans
- 1 can (8 ounces) pineapple tidbits, drained
- 1 jar (4-1/2 ounces) sliced mushrooms, drained
- 1 large onion, chopped
- 1 large green pepper, chopped
- 1/2 cup barbecue sauce
- 2 tablespoons soy sauce
- 1 garlic clove, minced
- 1/2 teaspoon salt
- 1/4 teaspoon pepper

In a skillet, brown beef; drain. Transfer to a 5-qt. slow cooker. Add remaining ingredients and mix well. Cover and cook on low for 4-8 hours or until bubbly. Serve in bowls. **Yield:** 6-8 main-dish or 12-16 side-dish servings.

Rich Spinach Casserole

Cook Time: 2-1/2 Hours

Vioda Geyer, Uhrichsville, Ohio

I discovered this recipe in an old cookbook. When I took the side dish to our church sewing circle, it was a big hit.

- 2 packages (10 ounces *each*) frozen chopped spinach, thawed and squeezed dry
- 2 cups (16 ounces) small-curd cottage cheese
- 1 cup cubed process cheese (Velveeta)
- 3/4 cup egg substitute
- 2 tablespoons butter, cubed
- 1/4 cup all-purpose flour
- 1/2 teaspoon salt

In a 3-qt. slow cooker, combine all ingredients; mix well. Cover and cook on low for 2-1/2 hours or until the cheese is melted. **Yield:** 8 servings.

Cheddar Spirals

(Pictured below)

Cook Time: 2-1/2 Hours

Heidi Ferkovich, Park Falls, Wisconsin

Our kids just love this and will sample a spoonful right from the slow cooker when they walk by. Sometimes I add cocktail sausages, sliced Polish sausage or cubed ham.

- 1 package (16 ounces) spiral pasta
- 2 cups half-and-half cream
- 1 can (10-3/4 ounces) condensed cheddar cheese soup, undiluted

Creamy Corn

Cheddar Spirals

- 1/2 cup butter, melted
- 4 cups (16 ounces) shredded cheddar cheese

Cook pasta according to package directions; drain. In a 5-qt. slow cooker, combine the cream, soup and butter until smooth; stir in the cheese and pasta. Cover and cook on low for 2-1/2 hours or until cheese is melted. **Yield:** 12-15 servings.

Creamy Corn

(Pictured above)

Cook Time: 4 Hours

Judy McCarthy, Derby, Kansas

A handful of ingredients and a slow cooker are all you'll need for this rich side dish. I first tasted it at a potluck with our camping club and I just had to get the recipe.

- 2 packages (16 ounces *each*) frozen corn
- 1 package (8 ounces) cream cheese, cubed
- 1/3 cup butter, cubed
- 1/2 teaspoon garlic powder
- 1/2 teaspoon salt
- 1/4 teaspoon pepper

In a slow cooker, combine all ingredients. Cover and cook on low for 4 hours or until heated through and cheese is melted. Stir well before serving. **Yield:** 6 servings.

Sweet Endings

Butterscotch Apple Crisp (p. 104)

Chapter 8

Hot Fudge Cake

Hot Fudge Cake

(Pictured above)

Cook Time: 4 to 4-1/2 Hours

Marleen Adkins, Placentia, California

A cake baked in a slow cooker may seem unusual, but chocolaty smiles around the table prove how tasty it is. Sometimes I substitute butterscotch chips for the chocolate.

1-3/4 cups packed brown sugar, *divided*
   1 cup all-purpose flour
   6 tablespoons baking cocoa, *divided*
   2 teaspoons baking powder
 1/2 teaspoon salt
 1/2 cup milk
   2 tablespoons butter, melted
 1/2 teaspoon vanilla extract
1-1/2 cups semisweet chocolate chips
1-3/4 cups boiling water
Vanilla ice cream

In a bowl, combine 1 cup brown sugar, flour, 3 tablespoons cocoa, baking powder and salt. In another bowl, combine the milk, butter and vanilla; stir into dry ingredients just until combined. Spread evenly into a 3-qt. slow cooker coated with nonstick cooking spray. Sprinkle with chocolate chips.

In a bowl, combine the remaining brown sugar and cocoa; stir in boiling water. Pour over batter (do not stir). Cover and cook on high for 4 to 4-1/2 hours or until a toothpick inserted near the center of cake comes out clean. Serve warm with ice cream. **Yield:** 6-8 servings.

Editor's Note: This recipe does not use eggs.

Slow-Cooker Berry Cobbler

Cook Time: 2 to 2-1/2 Hours

Karen Jarocki, Yuma, Arizona

I adapted my mom's yummy cobbler recipe for slow cooking, and this was the result. The summer months are hot here in Arizona, and thanks to this simple recipe, we can enjoy a homemade dessert without turning on the oven.

1-1/4 cups all-purpose flour, *divided*
   2 tablespoons plus 1 cup sugar, *divided*
   1 teaspoon baking powder
 1/4 teaspoon ground cinnamon
   1 egg, lightly beaten
 1/4 cup milk
   2 tablespoons canola oil
 1/8 teaspoon salt
   2 cups unsweetened raspberries
   2 cups unsweetened blueberries
   2 cups frozen vanilla yogurt, optional

In a bowl, combine 1 cup flour, 2 tablespoons sugar, baking powder and cinnamon. In another bowl, combine the egg, milk and oil; stir into dry ingredients just until moistened (batter will be thick). Spread batter evenly onto the bottom of a 5-qt. slow cooker coated with nonstick cooking spray.

In a bowl, combine salt and remaining flour and sugar; add berries and toss to coat. Spread over batter. Cover and cook on high for 2 to 2-1/2 hours or until a toothpick inserted into cobbler comes out without crumbs. Top each serving with 1/4 cup frozen yogurt if desired. **Yield:** 8 servings.

Crunchy Candy Clusters

Cook Time: 1 Hour

Faye O'Bryan, Owensboro, Kentucky

Before I retired, I used to take these yummy peanut butter bites to work for special occasions. They're so simple. I still make them for holidays because my family loves the cereal-and-marshmallow clusters.

   2 pounds white candy coating, broken into small pieces
1-1/2 cups peanut butter
 1/2 teaspoon almond extract, optional
   4 cups Cap'n Crunch cereal
   4 cups crisp rice cereal
   4 cups miniature marshmallows

Place candy coating in a 5-qt. slow cooker. Cover and cook on high for 1 hour. Add peanut butter. Stir in extract if desired. In a large bowl, combine the cereals and marshmallows. Stir in the peanut butter mixture until well coated. Drop by tablespoonfuls onto waxed paper. Let stand until set. Store at room temperature. **Yield:** 6-1/2 dozen.

Chocolate Pecan Fondue

(Pictured below)

Serve in Slow Cooker

Suzanne Cleveland, Lyons, Georgia

When our kids have friends sleep over, I like to surprise them with this chocolate treat. Sometimes we try different dippers such as marshmallows and pound cake.

> 1/2 cup half-and-half cream
> 2 tablespoons honey
> 9 ounces semisweet chocolate, broken into small pieces
> 1/4 cup finely chopped pecans
> 1 teaspoon vanilla extract
> **Fresh fruit and shortbread cookies**

In a heavy saucepan over low heat, combine cream and honey; heat until warm. Add chocolate; stir until melted. Stir in pecans and vanilla.

Transfer to a small slow cooker or warmed fondue pot and keep warm. Serve with fruit and cookies. **Yield:** 1-1/3 cups.

Granola Apple Crisp

Cook Time: 5 to 6 Hours

Barbara Schindler, Napoleon, Ohio

Tender apple slices are tucked beneath a sweet crunchy topping in this comforting, down-home dessert. For a change of pace, try replacing the apples with peeled and sliced pears or another fruit.

> 8 medium tart apples, peeled and sliced
> 1/4 cup lemon juice
> 1-1/2 teaspoons grated lemon peel
> 2-1/2 cups granola cereal with fruit and nuts
> 1 cup sugar
> 1 teaspoon ground cinnamon
> 1/2 cup butter, melted

In a large bowl, toss apples, lemon juice and peel. Transfer to a greased slow cooker. Combine cereal, sugar and cinnamon; sprinkle over apples. Drizzle with butter. Cover and cook on low for 5-6 hours or until the apples are tender. Serve warm. **Yield:** 6-8 servings.

Chocolate Pecan Fondue

Butterscotch Apple Crisp

Butterscotch Apple Crisp

(Pictured above and on page 100)

Cook Time: 5 Hours

Jolanthe Erb, Harrisonburg, Virginia

This sweet treat is a comforting way to warm up winter nights. The sliced apples are sprinkled with a tasty topping made with oats, brown sugar, cinnamon and convenient butterscotch pudding mix. Served with a big scoop of ice cream, the dessert is always well received.

- **6 cups sliced peeled tart apples (about 5 large)**
- **3/4 cup packed brown sugar**
- **1/2 cup all-purpose flour**
- **1/2 cup quick-cooking oats**
- **1 package (3-1/2 ounces) cook-and-serve butterscotch pudding mix**
- **1 teaspoon ground cinnamon**
- **1/2 cup cold butter**
- **Vanilla ice cream, optional**

Place the apples in a 3-qt. slow cooker. In a bowl, combine the brown sugar, flour, oats, pudding mix and cinnamon. Cut in the butter until the mixture resembles coarse crumbs. Sprinkle over the top of the apples. Cover and cook on low for 5 hours or until apples are tender. Serve crisp with ice cream if desired. **Yield:** 6 servings.

Fudgy Peanut Butter Cake

Cook Time: 1-1/2 to 2 Hours

Bonnie Evans, Norcross, Georgia

I clipped this recipe from a newspaper years ago, and we've enjoyed the yummy cake many times since. The house smells great while it's cooking. My husband and son enjoy the warm dessert with vanilla ice cream and nuts on top.

- **3/4 cup sugar, *divided***
- **1/2 cup all-purpose flour**
- **3/4 teaspoon baking powder**
- **1/3 cup milk**
- **1/4 cup peanut butter**
- **1 tablespoon vegetable oil**
- **1/2 teaspoon vanilla extract**
- **2 tablespoons baking cocoa**
- **1 cup boiling water**
- **Vanilla ice cream**

In a bowl, combine 1/4 cup sugar, flour and baking powder. In another bowl, combine the milk, peanut butter, oil and vanilla; stir into dry ingredients just until combined. Spread evenly into a slow cooker coated with nonstick cooking spray.

In a bowl, combine the cocoa and remaining sugar; stir in boiling water. Pour into slow cooker (do not stir). Cover and cook on high for 1-1/2 to 2 hours or until a toothpick inserted near the center of cake comes out clean. Serve warm with ice cream. **Yield:** 4 servings.

Dip into Dessert

Sweet dips served in the slow cooker can be just as much of a dessert treat as the usual brownie, piece of cake or slice of pie. From decadent Butterscotch Dip (recipe at right) to varieties featuring rich chocolate, these confections are a yummy way to top off a meal.

What's more, you can be creative and serve a variety of delicious dippers. Try an array of fresh fruits, such as apple and pear wedges, strawberries and cherries. (To help prevent cut apples and pears from browning, dip them into lemon or orange juice before serving.)

You could also offer sweet cinnamon chips, shortbread cookies or cubes of pound cake.

Butterscotch Dip

Cook Time: 45 Minutes

Jeaune Hadl Van Meter, Lexington, Kentucky

If you like butterscotch chips, you'll love this rum-flavored dip. It holds for up to 2 hours in the slow cooker, so it's great for parties and other get-togethers.

- **2 packages (10 to 11 ounces *each*) butterscotch chips**
- **2/3 cup evaporated milk**
- **2/3 cup chopped pecans**
- **1 tablespoon rum extract**
- **Apple and pear wedges**

In a mini slow cooker, combine butterscotch chips and milk. Cover and cook on low for 45-50 minutes or until chips are softened; stir until smooth. Stir in pecans and extract. Serve warm with fruit. **Yield:** about 3 cups.

Chocolate Bread Pudding

(Pictured below)

Cook Time: 2-1/4 to 2-1/2 Hours

Becky Foster, Union, Oregon

I love both chocolate and fresh-picked raspberries, so I was thrilled to come across this yummy recipe that combines the two. It's such a treat to lift the lid on the slow cooker and find this tempting dessert ready to enjoy. It's also a great way to use up your leftover bread from yesterday's dinner. I like to use egg bread for this recipe.

      6 cups cubed day-old bread (3/4-inch cubes)
  1-1/2 cups semisweet chocolate chips
      1 cup fresh raspberries
      4 eggs
  1/2 cup heavy whipping cream
  1/2 cup milk
  1/4 cup sugar
      1 teaspoon vanilla extract
  Whipped cream, optional

In a greased 3-qt. slow cooker, layer half of the bread cubes, chocolate chips and raspberries. Repeat layers. In a bowl, whisk the eggs, heavy whipping cream, milk, sugar and vanilla. Pour over the bread mixture.

Burgundy Pears

Cover and cook on high for 2-1/4 to 2-1/2 hours or until a thermometer reads 160°. Let stand for 5-10 minutes. Serve with whipped cream if desired. **Yield:** 6-8 servings.

Burgundy Pears

(Pictured above)

Cook Time: 3 to 4 Hours

Elizabeth Hanes, Peralta, New Mexico

These warm spiced pears elevate slow cooking to a new level of elegance, yet they're incredibly easy to make. Your family and friends will find it hard to believe that this fancy-looking dessert came from a slow cooker.

      6 medium ripe pears
  1/3 cup sugar
  1/3 cup Burgundy wine *or* grape juice
      3 tablespoons orange marmalade
      1 tablespoon lemon juice
  1/4 teaspoon ground cinnamon
  1/4 teaspoon ground nutmeg
  Dash salt
  Whipped cream cheese

Peel pears, leaving stems intact. Core from the bottom. Stand pears upright in a 5-qt. slow cooker. In a small bowl, combine the sugar, wine or grape juice, marmalade, lemon juice, cinnamon, nutmeg and salt. Carefully pour over pears. Cover and cook on low for 3-4 hours or until tender. To serve, drizzle pears with sauce and garnish with whipped cream cheese. **Yield:** 6 servings.

Chocolate Bread Pudding

Warm Strawberry Fondue

(Pictured below)

Serve in Slow Cooker

Sharon Mensing, Greenfield, Iowa

I need only a handful of ingredients for this fruit fondue. Serve it with grapes, bananas, berries and cake cubes.

> **1 package (10 ounces) frozen sweetened sliced strawberries, thawed**
> **1/4 cup half-and-half cream**
> **1 teaspoon cornstarch**
> **1/2 teaspoon lemon juice**
> **Angel food cake cubes and fresh fruit**

In a food processor or blender, combine the strawberries, cream, cornstarch and lemon juice; cover and process until smooth. Pour into a saucepan. Bring to a boil; cook and stir for 2 minutes or until slightly thickened. Transfer to a fondue pot or mini slow cooker; keep warm. Serve with cake and fruit. **Yield: 1-1/2 cups.**

Butterscotch Fondue

(Pictured below)

Serve in Slow Cooker

Folks of all ages will enjoy dipping into this yummy concoction from our Test Kitchen home economists.

> **1/2 cup butter, cubed**
> **2 cups packed brown sugar**
> **1 can (14 ounces) sweetened condensed milk**
> **1 cup light corn syrup**
> **2 tablespoons water**
> **1/4 cup English toffee bits *or* almond brickle chips**
> **1 teaspoon vanilla extract**
> **Angel food cake cubes and fresh fruit**

In a large saucepan, combine the butter, brown sugar, milk, corn syrup and water. Cook and stir over medium heat until smooth. Remove from the heat. Stir in toffee bits and vanilla. Transfer to a fondue pot or mini slow cooker; keep warm. Serve with cake and fruit. **Yield: 4 cups.**

Warm Fruit Compote

Cook Time: 2 Hours

Mary Ann Jonns, Midlothian, Illinois

I rely on the convenience of canned goods to prepare this old-fashioned treat. It's delicious any time of day.

> **2 cans (29 ounces *each*) sliced peaches, drained**
> **2 cans (29 ounces *each*) pear halves, drained and sliced**
> **1 can (20 ounces) pineapple chunks, drained**
> **1 can (15-1/4 ounces) apricot halves, drained and sliced**
> **1 can (21 ounces) cherry pie filling**

In a 5-qt. slow cooker, combine the peaches, pears, pineapple and apricots. Top with the cherry pie filling. Cover and cook on high for 2 hours or until heated through. Serve with a slotted spoon. **Yield: 14-18 servings.**

Butterscotch Fondue
Warm Strawberry Fondue

COOK TIME INDEX

This special index lists every recipe by cook time and page, so you can quickly find recipes that fit your schedule. Recipes are listed under the minimum cook time. Many have ranges, shown in parentheses, and may cook longer.

INGREDIENT INDEX

This handy index lists every recipe by food category and/or major ingredient, so you can easily locate recipes to suit your needs.